THE MODERNS AND THEIR WORLD

# THE
# MODERNS
# AND THEIR
# WORLD

WITH AN INTRODUCTION BY

SIR JOHN ROTHENSTEIN

DIRECTOR THE TATE GALLERY

LONDON

PHOENIX HOUSE LONDON

# INTRODUCTION

## by John Rothenstein

The paintings reproduced in this book have been selected* as a representative sample of modern art, of painting, that is to say, from Cézanne to our contemporaries, and they have been selected not only as distinguished works in their own kinds but also as illustrative of the most significant movements and aspects of modern painting. In introducing them I cannot, I think, do better than begin by issuing a gentle word of warning. They are not intended to suggest that the story of modern art is one of organic development, that it is, for all its complications, a fairly continuous story, a story of an art evolving according to its own inner logic and its own immanent dynamism. Even the lineage from Cézanne to Cubism and to Abstraction is not quite so clear and simple and respectable as is sometimes supposed. But it would appear to be an almost endemic assumption of the human mind that a common name stands for one and the same essential thing behind the appearances. "Modern art»» is by now a phrase sanctioned and sanctified by several decades of use. What more natural than to take it for granted that to the one phrase there does in fact correspond some one essential way of painting or of looking at the world that remains the same under no matter how many different manifestations and obeys the same inner compulsions of vision and feeling, if only we can be searching enough to discover them?

Of course the phrase "modern art" has not come into currency without a reason. It is not indeed to be thought of as a sort of hypostatized concept with a life of its own, a direction and a development independent of the attitudes and aspirations and ambitions and decisions of the fascinating and extremely idiosyncratic individuals some of whose paintings are reproduced in this volume. They are the agents of history and the servants neither of a Muse nor of movements or forces that use them. None the less there are family resemblances between them.

"Modern art", then, is by now a phrase of current usage, for modern art is something whose modernity contemporaries have been aware of in a manner perhaps unparalleled in history. Of course conservative critics, from Aristophanes and Plato onwards, have very frequently protested against innovations in the arts, "neotericism", and usually in moral terms; but until our own century, with a few exceptions (the most conspicuous, perhaps, being Turner), innovations and even revolutions have been regarded as being in some sense continuous with the past, or as at any rate taking place within a common discussable framework of ideas. But modern art is commonly thought of as being in essence revolutionary and, although in many particular respects antecedents can always be pointed to, revolutionary in the sense of making a complete break with the past. It may well be that it so appears only because we see it close up and that from the vantage point of a century hence, or even much less, our children will marvel at our want of percipience. It may well be so, and I think that it will be so, to the extent, at any rate, that it will be more clearly seen that the revolutionary art of our day, in spite of being in many respects formally discontinuous with our past, is by no means an arbitrary phenomenon, but that, on the contrary, it may

* With the exception of the British examples, which have been chosen by myself, the selection has been made by the publishers.

reasonably be correlated with certain antecedent changes in the relation of artist to society and in man's concept of himself and his place in nature.

To the contemporary identification of inspired and revolutionary art reference will be made later in these pages. But it is the case that the major painters of our own day have been almost all, at one time or another, innovators, absorbed in a new way of painting and a new way of looking at the world. Consider, for example, the painters with whom this book opens and whose work has been seminal for almost all the artists represented in it. Impressionist painters, themselves innovators, had a long struggle before they came to be accepted as respectable. But after neglect and execration, Impressionism succeeded in imposing itself as a great tradition of Western painting and like all successful innovations established for a time a sort of norm of vision. It imposed itself, too, for a time, as a central tradition, as a culminating stage in the effort to represent nature as nature really is. It might indeed be reasonably argued that until the end of the nineteenth century all disputes between rival "schools" of painting and between rival theorists and slogans were not disputes about whether nature should be "imitated" or not, but disputes about what is the proper concept of nature. Is nature universals immanent in particulars in such wise that particulars are accidental irrelevances that obscure the effulgence of form, or are the so-called accidents and the particularities so closely related to universals and to substances that only through their patient and individual scrutiny may reality be apprehended? In this and in other and subtler ways the concept of nature varied; the reference to nature was constant. The Impressionist innovations were themselves aims within a common framework of European painting, to represent, namely, the appearances of the world in the closest possible accord with the real and not the imagined or overladen facts of vision.

The Impressionists were a group of friends, very different one from the other, most of whom subsequently went their several ways; they were not a "school". Yet without undue simplification a major aim of theirs may be described as having been the representation, on the spot and there and then, of a casually chosen fragment of the natural world — any fragment — as the eye sees rather than as the mind apprehends. It was an art of the surfaces of things, of colour and light. The casual fragment of the visible world is inevitably lacking in the balance of subjects either deliberately selected or composed, so that the unity of the Impressionist picture is a unity of tone. It was primarily through truth to tone that this art was enabled to achieve a new kind of accuracy. The extraordinary brilliance of this group of men, and, one might add, their ravished delight in the appearances of the world, and their command of tone to give unity to any landscape or group of people, had the effect of inducing a new way of seeing, of seeing the world in terms of its surfaces and in terms of colour rather than of form, to the neglect of the rock and bone, the solid geometry beneath. And, of course, to carry conviction as representations of a fragment of the world caught here and now, in these particular conditions of light and weather, it was logical that Impressionist pictures should have the character of "impressions" or sketches carried out in broad suggestive brush-strokes.

Inevitably, these preoccupations excluded from the art of the Impressionists many of the qualities that characterized the work of the masters of the past. Painters who held their achievement in the highest regard and were proud to acknowledge themselves in their debt became none the less acutely aware how much of the totality of the world and of human nature had been left out. "They look for what is near the eye", said Gauguin, "and not at the mysterious heart of thought." Cézanne's celebrated remark that Impressionism must be made anew according to the art of the museums was a like expression of discontent at an art that lacked a certain massive reflectiveness and monumentality. Of the Impressionists themselves Monet was the most thoroughly consistent; Pissarro for a time made experiments under the guidance of Seurat, one of his own disciples; the rest were not for long satisfied with the Impressionist vision, and Renoir's bathers became not only linear but sculptural.

It was the rocky or bony structure of things that was restored most of all, then, by Cézanne's discontent. Not that this was in him an ideological programme, intellectual painter though he certainly was. Preoccupied with structure, he saw structure as structure of a visible world, a world, therefore, with surfaces, and these he sought strenuously to represent, and often with breath-taking success. The most reserved of artists, passionately defensive of his privacy, Cézanne's work does not easily yield its secrets. But it does convey how he saw the natural world, and it was the natural world that thus he saw.

Very heavy emphasis has been put by historians on these monumental qualities in the painting of Cézanne and on their influence on his followers and particularly the Cubists. Their consequences, we are told, have been to effect a return to classical structure and to geometry. That "the idea behind the modern movement in the arts is a return to the architectural or classical idea" is the opening proposition in a distinguished English critic's introduction to modern art. It is true enough that in the early analytic phase Cubist paintings were breaking down natural appearances into their component structures, and a new order of form was created, stark, dour, subtle, that increasingly, however, cut loose from the natural world. This programme, if programme it was, may be linked to the operations of Cézanne's intellect, if not, perhaps, to his senses and to his sketcher's technique. But the works of the Cubists, these brilliant creators of solid construction, of self-sufficient and satisfying form, turned out to be far removed from Cézanne's ideal "to make out of Impressionism something as solid and enduring as the art of the museums"; nor are they instances of architectural painting or of a classical ideal. Herwath Walden, the lively and perceptive editor of "Der Sturm", that fascinating art magazine which flourished before the First World War and a prime document of Expressionism, was inclined to call Cubism no less than Futurism and Abstraction by the name of Expressionism. To him they were more or less all one, dedicated as he was to the fight against realism and to the concept of the autonomous life of the picture. It is inaccurate but far from wild, for it has the merit of directing attention to the most salient feature of the work of Cézanne's Cubist followers, namely their highly idiosyncratic character, and to the liberty that their makers enjoy to create whatever forms they will. It is echoed by Ozenfant. "The Cubist painter", he wrote, "no longer sought to imitate. His object was to evoke emotions by the exhibition of coloured forms, which, not being comparable with aspects of reality, evaded the falsities inherent in *trompe l'œil* painting ... To paint true is to evoke in the observer exact sensations and appropriate feelings, and not fallaciously to imitate. And here we have one of the most important aspects of the modern attitude towards art, and to the Cubist goes the credit of having clearly stated it."

In this respect there is indeed a break between Cubism and Cézanne. The latter's adherence to his subject-matter was obstinate and passionate; the former created forms and related them independently of any reality external to them. The subject of the picture, Braque once said, is its poetical quality. And a picture is a thing-in-itself effiacious of itself, not a peep-hole into reality and not reminiscent of reality but its own autonomous reality. As I commented earlier, the lineage from Cézanne is not a simple one. On the other hand there is a lineage. Not a little of Picasso's extraordinary power lies in his astonishing ability to create new variations on traditional themes. Cézanne's ideas he brought to a series of surprising conclusions. But from these conclusions the logic of Abstraction is impeccable. Abstract art, with little of the emotion (and even violence) that can animate Cubist painting, removed on the whole — with the exception of some early Russian abstract painting — from the possibility of being plausibly labelled a sort of Expressionism, is an art none the less that affords deep satisfactions from the contemplation of forms in relation. It is no derogation of it to say that, intellectual though it is, its satisfactions are sensuous ones, primarily visual, or to complain that in the lack of public patronage abstract artists have been employed on easel pictures and not on the painting of walls. How enhancing of the act of living, as we go about our daily business, painted on walls of restaurant or conference room, would be the abstracts of Ben Nicholson — to name only the most illustrious of contemporary English abstract painters and the one who has brought this manner of painting to a perfection of elegance and of even dandyish finish.

The pity of it is, however, that like Cubism Abstraction has been enveloped and almost smothered in a mass of ideological theorising and built into a philosophy of nature and of knowledge and indeed of the unconscious. In particular they have both been treated as a sort of metaphysical painting that affords a superior insight into reality precisely because they are constructions unconcerned with the reality that we apprehend through our senses, and from the beginning, therefore, they have been associated with a view of the intrinsic superiority of non-representational painting that is indeed novel in the history of Europe. Fifty or a hundred years hence our children may wonder at our myopia, but for a contemporary it is none the less difficult not to share the impression that the characteristic art of our time is, in this respect, a product of a revolutionary change, of a radical discontinuity with our past. The history of European painting is largely a history of the persistence of two aims at grips with a resistent natural world — to represent as exactly as possible the painter's apprehension of the visible world and to evolve the perfect immanent forms of things and persons — and each aim has drawn power and vigour from its struggle with a resistent subject-matter; each has created its own images and its own attendant kinds of poetry. These aims crystallized in what for convenience are frequently termed the romantic and the classical ideals. From the Renaissance to the decline of Impressionism the interaction of these ideals has been constant. But from the end of the last century they have lost any compulsion or inspiration for great numbers of the most higly gifted artists. It is doubtful whether the invention of photography has had very much to do with this. It looks almost as if the very achievement of the Impressionists brought a sense of climax and, therefore, given the endemic restlessness of Western man, a sense of exhaustion and weariness and a feeling that a fresh start must somewhere be made. Yet there would seem to be other deeper and non-painterly causes at work. Whereas once it was taken for granted that an unremitting scrutiny of natural appearances might enhance both understanding and delight, and whereas once it was recognized that for a painter nature's appearances are in any case all the clues to or all the symbols of reality that he has, seeing that the world of the inner and the outer eye is all the visual world that as a painter he has; in our own time it is the opposite that is taken for granted : the majesty of the oak and the radiance of human beauty, and indeed their colours and their shapes, are but constructions of the human mind. "Out there" are atoms and the void, or the wild and whirling world of sense-data. What the eye sees is not what our forbears confidently thought that they saw. Nature and all the surfaces and the visible structure of nature are our "ideas", our theoretical or practical constructions, one degree removed from reality, which is the pure activity of spirit. This is indeed roughly how natural scientists have tended to talk for many decades. It is very much how philosophers have talked. On the Continent the effects of post-Kantian philosophical Idealism, in France and especially in Germany, have been pervasive: they have affected a whole climate of culture. But if the so-called object of knowledge or perception is not anything confronting the thinker or perceiver but is itself a construction of the thinker or perceiver, then clearly the old struggle in the "representation" of nature was a pointless wrestling; for the mind's own free creations or imaginings, independently of the natural order, are no less valid and informative, and indeed are more valid in that they are nearer to the creative heart of imagination and thought. If the appearances of the world are deceptive, then, and systematically deceptive, if they are no clue to reality and no image of it but are themselves man-made, the old aims of classicism and romanticism are both dissolved; it is equally foolish to represent or to idealize a mirage. Faced with natural beauty, wrote Benedetto Croce, man is exactly the mythical Narcissus at the pool.

This corrosion of confidence in the visible universe and the validity of our perceptions — and a certain dwindling of interest and curiosity — has had some obvious drawbacks. I shall refer only to two of them. What began in an atmosphere of revolution and was conducted through a renunciation of the world and the flesh has become in a way too easy and oddly devoid of tension — great art would seem to postulate a struggle with recalcitrance. It has also, in this same renunciation, renounced a limitlees repository of forms, as limitless, namely, as the visible universe. As a particularly perceptive historian has recently commented, "the abstract virtues of *The School of Athens* are richer, more numerous and more varied than those of any production of the contemporary abstract movement for the simple reason that Raphael was unhampered by any dread of natural appearances and found, effortlessly, in the fall of a cloak, in the moving tissues of the human body, a mine of material for the aesthetic manipulation of form." The view that naturalistic standards of representation have no aesthetic validity whatever, the same writer continues, was certainly a liberating force in the development of painting; but "the absolute abandonment of representation, which is no less than the abandonment of imagery, was not the logical next step in a process of enfranchisement".

From the discontent of Cézanne, then, with his Impressionist friends and from certain ideas about form implicit in his work and expressed in his sayings have derived notions that have gained a wide acceptance in the world of the masters of modern painting. There were also two other major figures of Post-Impressionism who fathered ideas, complementary and indeed over-lapping, that have exercised a decisive influence. The ideas of van Gogh and of Gauguin are in some respects very dissimilar but the total effect of their work has been in one direction. Both painters were conscious of the exclusion from Impressionism of the deeper human emotions; both, too, became aware that the Impressionist tonal technique, brilliantly adapted as it was to render the evanescent and, in the best and literal sense, the superficial, was ill fitted for the expression of the poetic and dramatic emotions of their own passionate natures. Gradually, therefore, both abandoned the Impressionist type of realism and evolved an art that was primarily symbolic and emotive.

In this art the functions of form and colour were to convey, symbolically but forcefully and sometimes violently, the painter's thought and feeling; sensuously, however, no less than symbolically. In van Gogh's later work colour does not primarily express form but makes an impact, even an assault, on our feelings, just by itself. Van Gogh was not an intellectual devisor of symbols or of anything else; all his life he remained an impassioned lover of the visible world — "Je mange de la nature" — with a sensuous joy in the colours that he used. What he saw he wrought more and more into an expression of his own despair, but his decorative handling of clear colour for its own sensuous delight is clear to see: "que c'est beau le jaune". Gauguin was more tempered and more deliberate. Painting, he wrote, "should make you think as music does, without the aid of images or ideas, simply by the mysterious relationships existing between our minds and the arrangements of colours and lines". Unsympathetic though he was to van Gogh's turbulent expressions of himself, he too saw compositions in terms primarily of patterns of juxtaposed and evocative colour and not all of tone, and it is these "mysterious relationships" that communicate the poetry and the drama.

"It must be remembered that any painting — before being a war-horse, a naked woman, or some anecdote — is essentially a flat surface covered with colours arranged in a certain order." This is not, of course, Gauguin but Maurice Denis summing up in 1890, in a well-known statement, the tenor of discussions among a group of young painters termed by Paul Serusier, one of them, the Nabis. (For Clive Bell it was a precise declaration of what Post-Impressionism is.) But Gauguin was a master particularly esteemed by this circle of painters — they included Serusier and Denis, the theorists of it, Bonnard, Vuillard, Roussel — and they were also among the first (they were painters, be it noted, not dealers) who sought out the works of Cézanne at *père* Tanguy's shop.

In an effort to keep a story tidy one speaks of groups and influences and uses labels; the words have their utility but they quickly become cant. The Nabis were a group of friends whose cohesion was loose and who shortly went their own ways; Vuillard and Bonnard belong to no grouping, but if one must group them they are latter-day children of the Impressionists rather than of anyone else. Similarly the Fauves were a short-lived association whose members went their several ways. Similarly, too, is it with "influences". When historians write of influences, what they are often describing is rather a shared way of looking at things that comes into being, sometimes mysteriously, and that one man, or a few, succeeds in crystallizing and in bringing to self-consciousness more than others. Not a little of Cézanne's struggle had been a strenuous marrying of his natural and spontaneous sense of flat pattern with his sense of solid form sustaining surfaces; both Gauguin and van Gogh loved the decorative quality of pure colour and pattern. It is not surprising that, as Maurice Denis subsequently wrote in 1895, the Nabis "preferred expression through decorative quality, through harmony of forms and colours, through the application of pigments, to expression through subject. They believed that for every emotion, for every human thought, there existed a plastic and decorative equivalent". In a similar strain the art critic of the *Mercure de France,* in an article entitled "Le symbolisme en peinture — Paul Gauguin" (March 1891), wrote that the work of art should be ideological, since its sole ideal is the expression of the idea; symbolical, because it expresses the idea through forms; subjective, because the object depicted is considered not as object but as the symbol of an idea suggested by the subject; and therefore, he concluded, decorative.

He added *emotivité*. It is the later work of van Gogh that may justly be considered as father to the Fauves — a circle of painters who got their name from a hostile critic in 1905; their leader, whose vision remained consistent throughout his long life, was Matisse, and the group included Dufy, Vlaminck, Derain and Rouault; Albert Marquet was also closely associated with it, and he had worked with Matisse towards this way of seeing and painting for several years. In van Gogh they appreciated the emotional impact and the sheer sensuous delight in slabs of pure colour; their work was a translation of the natural scene into terms of colour, and the brightest colour. They, too, believed in the autonomous life of the picture within the picture frame — "a flat surface covered with colour in a certain order" — and their joy in decoration was as keen as that of any Japanese artist. Indeed it was when Matisse subsequently affirmed that art is decoration that Rouault, the sombre suffering-haunted groping giant for whom painting is feeling, was induced to leave the Fauves. But above all, perhaps, their art was an art of exultant youth, zestful, full of confidence and verve, transported by a passionate and sensuous joy in the world around them. Not sensuous in the Impressionist sense, however; for it is essentially an imaginative art in which passionate apprehension transmutes and intensifies nature and creates new forms; in which, too, proportion and perspective exist for the sake of the life of the picture, to make, that is to say, its proportions and patterns sensuously more satisfying. Referring to his first acquaintance with Matisse's *Luxe, calme et volupté*, Dufy said of his experience in 1905 that he "understood all the new principles of painting, and impressionist realism lost its charm for me, as I contemplated the miracle of imagination introduced into design and colour. I immediately understood the new pictorial mechanics".

There was a German movement that is sometimes called Fauve but more often — although labels do not matter — Expressionist, for the latter was the more special direction in which it quickly developed. It was almost contemporary with the French but unconnected with it, though not, of course, unconnected with the work of van Gogh and Gauguin and more particularly the latter. I refer to the group in being at Dresden, termed "Die Brücke", during the decade before the First World War; the circle included Kirchner — more akin to the French than any of the others — Heckel, Schmidt-Rottluff, Pechstein, and (but for a year only) Nolde. August Macke, another painter temperamentally closer to the French, was more nearly linked by friendships to the much larger and more international group of advanced artists that came into vigorous life at Munich.

But here classifications begin seriously to break down, and not only because the personalities are as vigorous and various as they are brilliant. As a word used in contrast to Impressionism, Impressionism being conceived as an art that has to do with purely visual impressions, the surfaces of the world and the light that illumines and defines and unites them, Expressionism has a clear and intelligible meaning; it denotes an art, that is to say, concerned with the expression of ideas and emotions through the mediation of the things seen but using these things symbolically and emotively to express a vision of what reality, underneath appearances, is like. But yet is it really, after all, so clear? For in this sense of the word most major artists have been expressionists with some appreciable part of themselves. If we emend the description and understand the vision of what reality is like to be the expression of the artist's own personal feelings about things or the recreation of things according to the artist's personal mood, we are still no further from threatened vacuity. For this description, too, like the first, would cover not only a multitude of traditional artists but also painters at first sight as diverse as Fauves and Cubists and Surrealists and even some Abstractionists; it would include Picasso no less than Edvard Munch, Rouault no less than Paul Klee, Kandinsky no less than Chagall, Léger no less than Chirico, Stanley Spencer no less than Francis Bacon, Rivera no less than Soutine. But a description so comprehensive as to be unfalsifiable runs a risk of not being meaningful either.

In fact the Munich group of painters to which the name of "Der Blaue Reiter" was attached was a wide group with no programme other than to encourage *avant-garde artists*. It was also international. Kandinsky belonged to it, as did Paul Klee and Franz Marc, and almost from the beginning it was in touch with recent or contemporary painting in France, with the works of Cézanne, van Gogh, Gauguin, Picasso, Braque, Van Dongen, Matisse, Derain, Vlaminck, Rouault, Robert Delaunay, Rousseau. Its impetus was similar to that which animated Herwath Walden, for whom, as I earlier remarked, all contemporary painting merged into Expressionism — for the essence of painting was that it should express a personal vision or a personal emotion through paint. Kokoschka joined the staff of "Der Sturm", and Walden was responsible for exhibitions in Berlin that included works by Kandinsky, Chagall, Picasso and Léger. All forms of modern painting, then, were represented in Germany before the First World War, and it is characteristic of the Munich group that Marc, whose somewhat arbitrary use of colour had been "expressionistic" no less than symbolical, was moving into Abstraction when he was killed at Verdun.

Presumably the term "Expressionism" as a term of art history is intended to designate an intention and a method, but above all an emphasis; the intention, namely, of using the subject, whether representationally treated or not (in logic, at any rate, it does not matter), however transmuted or distorted, primarily or solely to express a personal and subjective emotion of the painter's individual and isolated self — I mean that he is not incidentally expressing his feelings while also saying something else about the world, but using his subject only to express his feelings; and with the intention goes a method, one, namely, of expressive lines and forms and particularly of colour emotively employed. It is not surprising that Expressionist manifestoes were couched also in the slogans of the "fight against representation" and denounced the "materialism" of the nineteenth century and of the Impressionists. The emphasis of Expressionist paintings, then, is on the expression of states of mind and the inner eye, and this often dramatically. The typical dramatization is naturally self-dramatization. It was accidental but to be expected — for Expressionism had its most vigorous roots in the Germanic countries and in Scandinavia — that the moods thus dramatically expressed should be not those of serenity or gaiety or happiness but predominantly those of a Dostoievskian and Strindbergian world: pessimism, tempestuousness, fear, anxiety, loneliness, isolation, violence, despair.

But just as the Abstract artists came to fall far short of the achievement of some of the early Cubists, of building, upon the prismatic forms of Cézanne, an art of solid, exactly defined form, and as the painters of pure form receded further and further not only from Cézanne's absorbed analysis of the visual world but also from his sense of structure and architecture; so, too, Expressionist painters proved progressively unable, after the early great days, to express anything beyond a narrow range of human emotions and a constricted vision of reality. For all that they translated much of the prevailing mood of the twentieth century, with the greater part of the human drama and with the poetry of life many of them came to be unwilling or unable to concern themselves. There are, of course, exceptions, and Munch, whose works could have been seen in Germany since the last decade of the nineteenth century and who affected the German Expressionists of this century only less than (though far less than) van Gogh and Gauguin, is pre-eminent among the exceptions. But an art of states of mind tends to be an introspective art in which to introspection is accorded a privileged access to reality, and it is natural, perhaps, that it should reflect little of the excitement of the human adventure and little of the older curiosity about the drama of life as it unfolds in one's own history and in the multitudinous aspects of human society that surround and shape personal histories. There would appear to have been a certain weakening of the life of the spirit, and of appetite and curiosity, parallel to and connected with the loosening of confidence in the reality of the visible world of which I spoke earlier in these pages.

Expressionism, I have urged, is a word that has a use in certain contexts but one which, as sometimes employed, approaches vacuity of meaning. It would be wrong, however, to attribute this simply to any loose-ness or imprecision in accounts of modern painting. As devised and used in the opening years of the present century the term tended to embrace all forms of Post-Impressionist art; not, however, arbitrarily. Earlier in this introduction I called in question the verdict that the idea behind the modern movement in the arts is a return to an architectural order and a classical ideal. For it seems to me that the distinguishing characteristic of the paint-ings actually produced since the great Post-Impressionists, on the Continent no less than in England, has been their overwhelmingly idiosyncratic character. There are family resemblances; there is no common essence. In part, no doubt, the reason is that in our own age it is an unconscious assumption that the great painter is one who innovates and does something markedly new, who is strikingly original. It has not always been so, and it is the exact opposite of any classical idea. But it is not surprising. In our restless century the possessor of superior gifts will be predisposed to attempt what has not been done before. But there is, I think, more to it than this. Most art propaganda of our time has been made in the forms of revolutionary language, of the imperative need to fight against realism or representation or tradition or convention, against any check on perfect freedom and the untrammelled self-expression of spirit. For many a decade this belligerency has been without a target; there are no more Bastilles to storm, and no restrictions on the absolute liberty of the artist to please himself. A quarter of a century ago Ozenfant put this very sharply and somewhat cruelly. "The individualism of today", he wrote, "is the spirit of liberty made subservient to SELF: the universe and mankind are at the feet of the individual. The one consideration is that the self be satisfied. The artist imagines, paints, writes just as he pleases, and much more for himself than for society... An anarchy of the Self: egotism, whether unconscious or conscious and directed... Yet this awareness of self had a certain fecundity; it, as it were, dug the grave of every privilege save that of man as God. It accepted nothing it had not personally verified; self was the centre of the world, and the world was fashioned in its image. Result, a thorough 'revision'. Good. But the converse of the romantic medal is a preference for what is extraordinary, and especially for what it remarkable. The Romanticist has in him something of the Exhibitionist."

"Cubism", wrote Guillaume Apollinaire, and he could have said the same of Abstraction, "differs from the old schools of painting in that it aims not at an art of imitation but at an art of conception, which tends to rise to the heights of creation." It is far from easy to find a sense in which the conceptions and the creations of Cubists may be properly said to be less exclusively the inventions of the painter's mind than the "literary" concepts of the Expressionists or the Surrealists. Both are like manifestations of the uninhibited expression of personality that is the prime characteristic of the art of the twentieth century.

In so far as this art is discontinuous with the art of its past, the principal reasons are outside the history of styles or art-forms; they are, rather, of a philosophical and a sociological nature. At the former I have already hinted. To some extent the latter are connected with the decline of patronage. When painters and sculptors are commissioned to do work that is going to be lived with, in a church or a public building or the patron's house, the subject is set and there are clients to be satisfied: there is a theme and a close relation between painter and society — and there is not likely to be, incidentally, much preference for the first aesthetic shock or the immediate lyrical or dramatic moment that we have come to expect of the uncommissioned easel picture seen in a studio or an art gallery. The uncommissioned easel picture has occasioned a new set of responses and preferences. But the obsolescence of patronage was itself accompanied, as was but natural, by the obsolescence of the apprentice system and its substitution by the art school. Conjointly these two factors have had a host of consequences. When paintings were commissioned and painters learned to paint in the studio of a master, in the discipline and tradition of a fairly homogeneous culture, there was no occasion for a man to undergo headaches or restlessness about what to paint or how to paint it, or to be obsessed with creative freedom. The questions settled themselves. Nor was he made aware through photography of forms and styles culled from every corner of the globe and from most centuries of recorded time — of the ubiquitous gallery that André Malraux has called the *musée imaginaire*. Artists have drawn inspiration from engravings and from museums ever since the Renaissance, but how comparatively few and homogeneous, before the discovery of photography, these were. A few prints after paintings by Michelangelo were enough to produce an intense and lasting impression on the imagination of Blake. But with the dissemination of photographs and the development of art galleries there came to be available, in our century, a multiplicity of art forms that enabled painters to extend the range of their aesthetic experience far beyond their personal experience of nature and man. It has been argued that photography and museums have also facilitated the inferring of something called the pure aesthetic experience — have eased the implication that, as one of our most intelligent historians has described it, "the value of art depends on a mysterious essence or elixir which can be isolated, almost tapped off from the body or husk of the work; and this elixir alone is worthy of pursuit."

The concept of aesthetic essence has certainly played a large part in the thinking of writers about aesthetics and naturally, therefore, in the writings of critics. From it, it may well be, the notion drew some of its strength that, as a distinguished American scholar has put it, "since resemblance to nature is at best superfluous and at worst distracting, it might as well be eliminated". It has tended to set a premium on non-representational work, and on work that used nature as a starting point for a detached study in extraneous formal arrangements. Even in the work of Expressionists — for they, too, as we saw, were on the whole systematically opposed to representation in the interests of complete subjectivity and freedom of creativity — it has tended to an undervaluing of the image, and this may be why Surrealist art was felt by many as a liberation and as a restoration to painting of a poetry that it had come to lack. In contemporary painting we are less shy of evocative images, whether transmuted or not, than once we were.

It is an interesting and significant fact that just as the studied disinterest in or positive antipathy to representation may be correlated with pivotal doctrines in both English and Continental philosophy, so too the modern obsession with creative freedom and the liberation of the self from the clutter and trammels of nature and of concepts, both theoretical and practical, is correlatable with some key doctrines of Continental philosophy, most markedly, perhaps, of that of Croce, who recapitulates so many of its themes; for Continental philosophy since Kant has been, on the whole, variations of a philosophical Idealism which, as I commented earlier but as is clear to see, has been formative of an entire culture. The same philosophy has underwritten, too, some familiar kindred and overlapping axioms: the assumption, for instance, of what has been termed the revolutionary principle, or the faith that revolutionary vision means spiritual progress, and the doctrine of a pure essence of art and of aesthetic essence as a primal, prelogical, autonomous mode of the self-expression of spirit prior to all its other activities.

People live in contexts and painters paint in contexts, and therefore cultural and sociological considerations are relevant to the understanding of what happens in painting. For the same reason it is not amiss to attend to historical groupings of painters, Fauves, the Brücke, Cubists and the rest, or even to historical classifications like that resumed in the term "Expressionism". But this I have done with many reserves. There were these groupings; there were, that is to say, at certain times and places, friends associating together and confirming one another in ideas and antipathies, enthusiasms and sympathies. But in the history of painting, and particularly in that of modern painting, groupings are deceptive; as classifications they can be thoroughly misleading. They are more ephemeral than at first they appeared to be, and more fortuitous in their composition; they shift and dissolve under scrutiny. Unlike the individuals who compose them they have no hard core, no common personality or individuality. In our age there are no homogeneous traditions to which original artists might plausibly be attached; they exist by virtue of their individual selves. Art history aims at tidiness and therefore likes categories. The original modern artist does not easily fit into any of them. For a time some of them were indeed associated together and animated one another, as were the Brücke group and to a lesser degree the Fauves and to a still lesser extent the Nabis; but Schmidt-Rottluff is very different from Nolde, Dufy from Matisse, Bonnard from Denis, Macke from Kokoschka. All of them have looked with interest, sometimes with absorbed and usually with respectful interest, at the work of the others, as Klee and Chagall, for instance, at the paintings of the Cubists. But neither Klee nor Chagall fits into a category, although they have been claimed for several. Picasso is a Proteus, the prodigiously gifted master all styles and media; Rouault is monolithically the same. Some have changed course; some, like Matisse or Bonnard, have worked with a serene consistency.

In fact the history of the modern masters is a history of the most extreme manifestation of the liberal humanist tradition in Western Europe — a tradition that, as the Communists were quick to recognise when they immured such examples of modern painting as had been collected in Russia, has always put a high value on individual personality and on the privilege of self-expression. In modern painting it is a supreme value, and this is why an essay such as this inevitably began with a *caveat*. There is no organic development of modern painting according to some immanent inner logic and dynamism; there are the works of a succession of highly gifted and original painters. Of course they live in a cultural *milieu* and their works affect one another; there are family likenesses, to which I have indeed drawn attention. But the paintings are in the first place and all the time the self-expressions of individuals for whom the realization of the personal vision is among their highest rights and duties as artists.

## BACON, FRANCIS

Born in Dublin 28 October 1910. Spent his youth in Ireland. Began to paint, without instruction, in 1930. Strongly influenced by Surrealism and by the Cubism of Picasso. Depicts mainly the macabre, the terrible and the sensational, and every kind of catastrophe, working from early films and newspaper photographs. Exhibited at the UNESCO International Exhibition of Modern Painting in Paris, 1946. 1949 first one-man exhibition at the Hanover Gallery, London. 1950 visited Egypt and Africa, and in 1952 paid a second visit to Africa. Exhibitions held at the Venice Biennale in 1954, London 1955 and Paris 1957.

*Literature:* S. Hunter, Francis Bacon, "The anatomy of Horror", in: Magazine of Art, XLV, 1, 1952. — Masters of British Painting 1800—1950, Introduction and Notes by A. C. Ritchie, New York 1956.

## BECKMANN, MAX

Born in Leipzig, 12 February 1884. 1899 began to study painting under Frithjof Smith in Weimar. 1903—1904 visited Paris and Florence. Exhibitions in 1906 at the Berlin Sezession and the Künstlerbund in Weimar; was awarded the "Villa Romana" Prize for the latter. Married for the first time and settled in Berlin. 1908 visited Paris. Member of the Berlin Sezession for a short time. 1914—1915 military service in the medical corps during the First World War. 1915—1933 lived in Frankfurt a. M. 1924 married the daughter of the painter von Kaulbach. 1925 became Professor at the Art School in Frankfurt a. M. and Director of the Painting Department. Important Exhibitions in Mannheim, Basle and Paris 1928—1932: awarded the Carnegie Prize. 1933 was dismissed by the Nazis and moved to Berlin. Created the first great triptychs. 1937—1947 lived as an emigré in Amsterdam. 1947 visited Nice, and later went to America where he taught at the Washington University in St. Louis. In New York from 1949 where he taught at the Brooklyn Art School. Travelled extensively in America. Awarded the Carnegie and Biennale Prizes, and an Honorary Doctorate of the Washington University, St. Louis. Died in New York 27 December 1950. The works of Beckmann include numerous graphic works, drawings, sculptures and poetry, as well as paintings.

*Literature:* C. Glaser, J. Meier-Graefe, W. Fraenger und W. Hausenstein, Max Beckmann, München 1924. — J. B. Neumann, Max Beckmann, New York 1931. — W. Schöne, Max Beckmann, Berlin 1947. — F. Roh, Max Beckmann als Maler, München 1947. — B. Reifenberg und W. Hausenstein, Max Beckmann, München 1949. — Max Beckmann, Tagebücher 1940—1950, hg. von E. Göpel, München 1955. — G. Busch, Max Beckmann, München 1960.

## BOCCIONI, UMBERTO

Born in Reggio-Calabria 19 October 1882. 1898 went to Rome where he met the painter Gino Severini and Giacomo Balla who introduced him to the principles of Impressionism and Neo-Impressionism. 1902—1904 studied in Paris and Berlin visited St. Petersburg. Lived in Milan from 1907; important meeting with Marinetti, the founder of Futurism. The first Futurist Manifesto appeared in the "Figaro" 20 February 1909. 1911 in Paris again, where he became acquainted with Apollinaire and the Cubist painters. In the following year he exhibited at the first Futurist exhibition at the Galerie Bernheim-Jeune in Paris, his Futurist sculptures being exhibited in Paris in 1913. Volunteered for military service in 1915 and died of injuries 17 August 1916.

*Literature:* F. T. Marinetti, Umberto Boccioni, Milano 1924. — M. Valsecchi, U. Boccioni, Venezia 1950. — G. C. Argan, Boccioni, Roma 1953.

## BONNARD, PIERRE

Born in Fontenay-aux-Roses (Seine) 13 October 1867, the son of a high-ranking official at the War Ministry. Began to study law before turning to art in 1888. Studied at Julian's where he met Sérusier, Denis, Vuillard and others. Joined the "Nabis" circle. His early works are mainly decorative designs, lithographs for the Revue Blanche and illustrations for "Parallèlement" by Verlaine, 1900 and "Daphnis and Chloé" by Longus, 1902. Exhibited at the first Salon d'Automne. 1907—1911 visited Belgium, Holland, England, Italy, Spain and Tunisia. 1912—1938 lived alternately in the Seine Valley, the South of France and on the North Sea coast. After 1940 lived in retirement at Le Cannet, near Cannes, where he died 23 January 1947. The paintings of Bonnard, whose principal theme is woman, include still-life, portraits, interiors and landscapes.

*Literature:* Ch Terrasse, Bonnard, Paris 1927. — P. Courthion, Bonnard, Lausanne 1945. — G. Jedlicka, Bonnard, Zürich 1947. — J. Rewald, Pierre Bonnard, New York 1948. — G. Jedlicka, Pierre Bonnard. Ein Besuch, Erlenbach-Zürich 1949. — T. Natanson, Le Bonnard que je propose, Genève 1951. — H. Rumpel, Bonnard, Bern 1952.

## BRAQUE, GEORGES

Born in Argenteuil near Paris 13 May 1882. Spent his youth in Le Havre; apprenticed to his father as a decorative painter. Has lived in Paris since 1900. 1902—1904 studied at the Ecole des Beaux-Arts and the Académie Humbert. 1906 with Friesz in Antwerp; later turned to Fauvism. 1908 went to L'Estaque near Marseilles and under the influence of Cézanne, like Picasso, painted his first Cubist pictures. The pictures painted during this period were rejected by the Salon d'Automne but were exhibited at Kahnweiler's. Analytical Cubism. 1911—1912 period of papier collé and change to synthetic Cubism. Served in the First World War and was discharged after having been seriously wounded. In the following years he introduced more representational elements into his Cubist style. Lived in the Pyrenees during the Second World War, returning to Paris in 1944. 1948 awarded a Biennale Prize. Paints mainly still life, and, since 1936, nudes and interiors: also graphic artist and sculptor.

*Literature:* C. Einstein, Georges Braque, Paris 1934. — J. Paulhan, Braque le Patron, Genève 1946. — J. Grenier, Braque. Peintures 1909—1947, Paris 1948. — S. Fumet, Braque, Paris n. d. — H. R. Hope, Georges Braque, New York 1949. — A. Lejard, Braque, Paris 1949. — F. Laufer, Braque, Bern 1954. — M. Gieure, Braque, Paris 1956. — J. Richardson, Braque, London 1959. — J. Leymarie, Braque, Genève 1961.

## CAMPIGLI, MASSIMO

Born in Florence 4 July 1895. First worked as a journalist in Milan, but at the age of 24 turned to painting which he taught himself. In Paris, where he gained his first successes, he was greatly influenced by Picasso and Léger, but archaic Greek, Etruscan and Roman art were also decisive factors in his development as a painter. Travelled extensively in Europe. Lived in Milan during the Second World War. Important exhibition at the Venice Biennale 1948. Campigli has been living in Paris since 1948.

*Literature:* R. Carrieri, Massimo Campigli, Milano 1941. — R. Franchi, Massimo Campigli, Milano 1944. — M. Raynal, Campigli, Paris 1949.

## CARRA, CARLO

Born in Quargnento (Piedmont) 11 February 1881. Was engaged on decorative compositions until his entry into the Brera Academy in Milan. Visited Paris and London. Met Marinetti and Boccioni and was a joint founder of Futurism. 1910 signed the Manifesto of Futurist Painting. 1911 during his second visit to Paris he met Apollinaire and the Cubists. 1915 turned to metaphysical painting in Ferrara under the influence of de Chirico. After the First World War joined the "Valori Plastici" group. His style of painting shows the influence of the early Florentines, particularly Massaccio. In the 1930s visited Munich, Dresden, Prague, Algeria, Malta, and Sicily. One-man exhibition at the Venice Biennale 1950. Carrà was also an etcher, illustrator and writer.

*Literature:* P. M. Bardi, Carrà e Soffici, Milano 1930. — R. Longhi, Carlo Carrà, Milano 1937. — G. Pacchioni, Carlo Carrà, Milano 1945.

## CEZANNE, PAUL

Born in Aix-en-Provence 19 January 1839, Cézanne is the most important forerunner and actual founder of modern painting. Had a sound humanist education. Friendly with Zola. In accordance with the wishes of his father he began to study law, but in 1861 turned to painting which he studied at the Académie Suisse. Became acquainted with Pissarro. Having been refused admission to the Ecole des Beaux-Arts he returned to Aix disappointed and worked for a short time in his father's business. 1862 second stay in Paris, where he was friendly with the Impressionists and became acquainted with Manet. 1864—1870 spent his time alternately in Paris and Aix. In the following years he worked in the vicinity of the capital and exhibited at the Impressionist exhibitions of 1874—1877. After 1882 lived mainly in l'Estaque and Aix. 1886 break with Zola. 1887 exhibited in Brussels with the "Groupe de XX". The following year he met van Gogh, Gauguin and Emile Bernard in Paris. Returned to Aix, where he remained for the rest of his life, except for short periods. First exhibition at Vollard's in Paris 1895. Important exhibitions at the Salon d'Automne and the Salon des Indépendants 1904 and 1905. Died 22 October 1906.

*Literature:* A. Vollard, Paul Cézanne, Paris 1914. — J. Meier-Graefe, Cézanne, London/New York 1927. — L. Venturi, Cézanne, sont art, son œuvre, 2 vol., Paris 1936. — M. Raynal, Cézanne, Paris 1936. — F. Novotny, Cézanne und das Ende der wissenschaftlichen Perspektive, Wien 1938. — J. Rewald, Paul Cézanne, sa vie, son œuvre, son amitié pour Zola, Paris 1939. — A.-C. Burnes and V. de Mazio, The Art of Cézanne, New York 1939. — B. Dorival, Cézanne, Paris 1948. — Meyer Schapiro, Paul Cézanne, Köln n. d.


## CHAGALL, MARC

Born in Witebsk, Russia, 7 July 1887. Apprenticed first to an academic painter, and in 1907 studied painting in St. Petersburg. 1910—1914 in Paris where he became friendly with the painters La Fresnaye, Delaunay and Modigliani. First big exhibition in the "Sturm" in Berlin. Returned to Russia. In 1917 he founded an Academy of Fine Arts in Witebsk, and in 1919 was commissioned to paint murals for the Jewish Theatre in Moscow. 1922 went to Berlin and thence to Paris where Vollard commissioned him to illustrate Gogol's "Dead Souls" and La Fontaine's "Fables". 1931 visited the Middle East, and 1935 Poland. Emigrated to America in 1941. 1945 designed the décors and costumes for Stravinsky's ballet "The Firebird". A big exhibition was held in New York in 1946 and was shown in the following year in Amsterdam and London. Returned to France in 1947. Since 1949 has remained permanently in Vence in the South of France where he is engaged on ceramics as well as painting.

*Literature:* A. Efross und J. Tugendhold, Die Kunst Marc Chagalls, Potsdam 1921. — W. George, Marc Chagall, Paris 1928. — A. Salmon, Chagall, Paris 1928. — L. Venturi, Marc Chagall, New York 1945. — J. J. Sweeney, Marc Chagall, New York 1946. — J. Lassaigne, Chagall, Genève 1951. — G. Schmidt, Chagall, Basel 1955. — L. Venturi, Chagall, Genève 1956. — F. Meyer, Marc Chagall. Das graphische Werk, Stuttgart 1957.


## CHIRICO, GIORGIO DE

Born in Volo, Greece, 10 July 1888, of Italian parents. Studied painting in Athens and later in Munich where he was influenced by Böcklin and Marées. 1911—1915 in Paris where he met Picasso and Apollinaire's circle. First metaphysical pictures. 1915 met Carrà in Ferrara, and Carrà, under his influence, also turned to metaphysical painting. In Rome and Florence in the following year: joined the "Valori Plastici" group. Gradual change to romantic Neoclassicism. 1924 in Paris again, where he reverted to his metaphysical style. 1925 exhibited at the Surrealist exhibition in Paris. 1929 publication of his novel "Hebdomeros". Designs for Krenek's opera "Oreste" in Berlin. 1933 began the murals for the Palazzo della Triennale in Milan. 1935—1938 in Paris again, also in Milan, Florence and Rome. His later work is characterized by a return to an academic style of painting.

*Literature:* W. George, Giorgio de Chirico, Paris 1928. — B. Ternovetz, Giorgio de Chirico, Milano 1928. — Lo Duca, Giorgio de Chirico, Milano 1936 (Nuova edit. 1945). — J. Th. Soby, The early Chirico, New York 1941. — R. Carrieri, Giorgio de Chirico, Milano 1942. — J. Faldi, Giorgio de Chirico, Venezia 1949.


## DALI, SALVADOR

Born in Figueras, near Barcelona, 11 May 1904. 1921—1924 studied art at the Academy of Fine Arts in Madrid. Influenced by Cubism and particularly by the metaphysical painting of de Chirico and Carrà. 1928 visited Paris where he met Picasso and the Surrealist painters and writers. Worked on films and the illustration of Lautréamonts "Chants de Maldoror". 1934 first visit to America. 1937 visited Italy. The Italian Renaissance, Raphael and the Baroque have had particular influence on his painting. 1940 settled in America. 1941 exhibition at the Museum of Modern Art in New York. 1950 spent some time in Rome before returning to Spain.

*Literature:* J. Th. Soby, Salvador Dali, New York 1946.


## DELAUNAY, ROBERT

Born in Paris 12 April 1885. 1902 began to paint in the studio of a decorative painter. 1904 spent some time in Brittany where he became acquainted with the Pont-Aven School. 1905 Neo-Impressionist period. 1910 exhibited at the Salon des Indépendants. 1911 associated with the "Blue Rider" group founded by Kandinsky and Marc. 1912 period of Orphic Cubism. 1913 went with Apollinaire to Berlin and exhibited at the "Sturm". In Spain and Portugal during the First World War. 1918 décors for Diaghilev's ballet "Cléopatra". 1921 returned to Paris. 1937 important commission for the decoration of the Railway and Airway Palaces at the Paris World's Fair. 1939 first "Réalités Nouvelles" exhibition at the Galerie Charpentier. Died in Montpellier 25 October 1941.

*Literature:* F. Gilles de la Tourette, Robert Delaunay, Paris 1950.


## DEMUTH, CHARLES

Born in Lancaster 1883. Paralysed from childhood. First studied art at the Pennsylvania Academy of Fine Arts in Philadelphia, and in 1904 in Paris. Influenced by Marin. Shows leaning towards the Realist masterpieces. 1926 big exhibition at the Intimate Gallery in New York. Died 23 October 1935. Memorial exhibition in New York 1938.

*Literature:* A. E. Gallatin, Charles Demuth, New York 1927. — W. Murrell, Charles Demuth, New York 1931. — A. C. Ritchie, Charles Demuth, New York n. d.


## DENIS, MAURICE

Born in Grandville 25 November 1870. 1888 entered Julian's in Paris, where he met Bonnard, Vuillard and Sérusier with whom he founded the "Nabis" group. 1893 carried out decorations for the Théâtre de l'Oeuvre and various churches. Of the many countries visited by Denis in Europe, the Near East and America, Italy was that which influenced him most. 1908 taught at the Académie Ranson. 1912 began the decorations for the Théâtre des Champs-Elysées. 1919 founding of the Ateliers d'Art Sacré in Paris. Died in Saint-Germain-en-Laye 3 November 1943.

*Literature:* F. Fosca, Maurice Denis, Paris 1924. — M. Brillant, Maurice Denis, Paris 1929. — S. Barazetti, Maurice Denis, Paris 1945. — P. Jamot, Maurice Denis, Paris 1945.

## DERAIN, ANDRE

Born in Chatou 10 June 1880. Began to study engineering which he soon gave up for painting. Studied painting at the Académie Carrière, where he met Matisse. Friendly with Vlaminck. 1901 influenced by the paintings of van Gogh. 1904 continued his studies at Julian's. Worked in the South with Matisse and exhibited at the Fauve exhibition at the Salon d'Automne. From 1907 was also engaged in wood engraving, sculpture and ceramics. 1908 came under the influence of Cézanne and Cubism. 1910 spent some time in Cagnes. Visited Spain where he met Picasso. 1912 beginning of the "Gothic" period. 1914 until 1918 military service. 1920—1930 visited the South and Italy: big exhibition at the Paul Guillaume galleries. Died 1954.

*Literature:* H. Daniel, André Derain, Leipzig 1920. — A. Salmon, André Derain, Paris 1924. — A. Basler, Derain, Paris 1931. — J. Leymarie, André Derain, Genève 1948. — G. Hilaire, Derain, Genève 1959.

## DUFY, RAOUL

Born in Le Havre 3 June 1877. Studied painting in Le Havre and after 1900 at the Ecole des Beaux-Arts in Paris. First influenced strongly by the Impressionists and van Gogh. 1905 under the influence of Matisse became interested in Fauvism. 1906 exhibited for the first time at the Salon d'Automne. 1907 under the influence of Cézanne adopted a Cubist style of painting. 1908 worked with Braque in L'Estaque, and later visited Munich. 1911 was encouraged by the tailor Poiret to take up textile designing. After 1920 also produced tapestries and ceramics. 1922 visited Sicily, and 1925 Morocco. 1937 carried out the extensive decorations for the Electricity Palace at the Paris World's Fair, also decorations for the Palais de Chaillot. 1940 in Perpignan. 1950 went to Boston to undergo special treatment for rheumatoid arthritis. 1951 returned to France and settled in Forcalquier in 1952. Awarded the First Prize at the Venice Biennale. Died 23 March 1953.

*Literature:* M. Berr de Turique, Raoul Dufy, Paris 1930. — J. Cassou, Raoul Dufy, Poète et Artisan, Genève 1946. — M. Gauthier, Raoul Dufy, Paris 1949. — C. Roger-Marx, Raoul Dufy, Paris 1950. — P. Courthion, Raoul Dufy, Genève 1951. — G. Besson, Raoul Dufy, Paris 1953. — J. Lassaigne, Dufy, Genève 1954.

## ENSOR, JAMES

Born in Ostend 13 April 1860. 1877 entered the Brussels Art Academy. Returned to Ostend, where he remained for the rest of his life. 1883 member of the group "Les XX", which in 1884 exhibited for the first time in Brussels. 1930 King Albert of Belgium raised Ensor to the nobility. Died in Ostend 19 November 1949. Ensor's main works date from 1890; they are, besides landscapes and portraits, interiors and masquerade scenes of a mock-burlesque type — also graphic works. Also experimented as a writer and composer.

*Literature:* F. Cuypers, James Ensor. L'homme et l'œuvre, Paris 1926. — P. Colin, James Ensor, Leipzig 1931. — P. Fierens, James Ensor, Paris 1943. — F. Cuypers, Aspects et propos de James Ensor, Bruges 1946. — R. Avermate, James Ensor, Antwerpen 1947. — F. Fels, James Ensor, Genève 1947.

## ERNST, MAX

Born in Brühl, near Cologne, 2 April 1891. Studied history of art in Bonn and later changed to painting, without instruction. 1913 exhibited at the first German Autumn Salon in Berlin and later went to Paris. 1914—1918 military service. 1919 in Cologne, with Arp and Baargeld, he founded the "Dada" group from which eventually emerged the "Schammade". 1922 in Paris where he contributed to "Littérature" and the illustration of Eluard's works. Joint-founder of Surrealism: 1925 first Surrealist exhibition in Paris. Until the Second World War was also a writer, designer of theatre decorations, decorative painter and illustrator. 1939—1940 interned in the South of France. 1941 until 1945 lived in New York, and later in Sedona (Arizona) except for long visits to Paris.

*Literature:* Max Ernst, Oeuvres de 1919—1936, Paris 1937. — J. Bousquet et M. Tapié, Max Ernst, Paris 1950. — L. Pretzell, Max Ernst, Brühl 1951.

## FEININGER, LYONEL

Born in New York 17 July 1871. 1887 began to study music in Hamburg but decided in the same year to take up painting. 1887—1893 studied painting in Hamburg, Berlin and Paris. 1893—1906 worked in Berlin as an illustrator for "Ulk" and the "Lustigen Blätter". Spent two years in Paris working for the Chicago Sunday Tribune. 1908 in Berlin. 1911 while visiting Paris he became acquainted with Delaunay and Cubism. 1913 exhibited at the "Blue Rider" exhibition at the First German Autumn Salon in Berlin. 1919—1933 taught at the Bauhaus in Weimar and later in Dessau. 1924 together with Kandinsky, Klee and Jawlensky founded the "Blue Four" group. 1936 returned to America. Commissioned to paint frescoes for the 1939 New York World's Fair. 1944 big exhibition at the Museum of Modern Art in New York. Died 13 January 1956.

*Literature:* A. J. Schardt and A. H. Barr, Lyonel Feininger, New York 1944. —D. Miller, Lyonel Feininger, New York 1944.

## GAUGUIN, PAUL

Born in Paris 7 June 1848, the son of a journalist. 1851—1855 in Lima with his great uncle. 1856 the Gauguin family settled in Orleans. Entered the marines. 1871 employed at the Bertin Bank in Paris. Married a Danish woman. Attempted to paint at first in the style of Pissarro. 1883 gave up his post at the Bank and devoted himself wholly to painting. Moved to Copenhagen with his family, but soon left them and returned to Paris. First stay in Pont-Aven in Brittany. On his return to Paris he made the acquaintance of van Gogh. 1887 sailed for Panama but on account of a typhoid epidemic went on to Martinique. 1888 second stay in Pont-Aven. Became the head of a school of painters who strove, unlike the Impressionists, for synthesis. In the Autumn of 1888 he worked with van Gogh in Arles, until van Gogh, in a fit of madness, tried to kill him, when he left Arles and returned to Paris. 1891 auctioned 30 pictures and used the proceeds to pay for the journey to the South Sea Island of Tahiti. Publication of his autobiographical novel "Noa Noa". 1893 exhibited the Tahiti pictures at Durand-Ruel in Paris. During the last great phase of his artistic work he suffered considerable privations and illness. 1901 moved to the island of La Dominique, where he died on 8 May 1903 in the greatest misery.

*Literature:* Ch. Morice, Paul Gauguin, Paris 1919. — Ch. Chassé, Gauguin et le groupe de Pont-Aven, Paris 1921. — W. Barth, Paul Gauguin, Basel 1929. — A. Alexandre, Paul Gauguin, sa vie et le sens de son œuvre, Paris 1930. — J. Rewald, Gauguin, Paris 1938. — L. Hautecœure, Gauguin, Paris 1938. — H. Graber, Paul Gauguin, nach eigenen und fremden Zeugnissen, Basel 1946. — M. Malingue, Gauguin, Le Peintre et son œuvre, Paris 1948. — H. Read, Gauguin, London 1949. — G. Schmidt, Gauguin, Bern 1950. — Ch. Estienne, Gauguin, Genève 1953. — R. Goldwater, Paul Gauguin, Köln 1957. — R. Hugghe, Gauguin, Paris 1959.

## GILMAN, HAROLD

Born in Rode, Somerset, 11 February 1876, the son of a clergyman. Attended schools in Abingdon, Rochester and Tonbridge. 1894 entered Brasenose College, Oxford. 1896 began to study art at the Hastings Art School, transferring the follow year to the Slade School. During a visit to Spain in 1904 he was deeply impressed by the paintings of Velazquez and Goya, of which he made copies in the Prado. Entered the Fitzroy Street Circle founded by Sickert. The first Post-Impressionist exhibition in 1910 made a deep impression on him. In Paris, where he met Ginner, he changed the tones of his palette under the influence of van Gogh, Gauguin, Signac and Cézanne. 1931 elected first President of the London Group. Taught for a short time at the Westminster School and later founded his own painting school in collaboration with Ginner. Died in London 12 February 1919. Painted mainly interiors, portraits and landscapes.

*Literature:* W. Lewis and L. F. Fergusson, Harold Gilman, An Appreciation, London 1919. — A. Gwynne-Jones, Portrait Painters, London 1950.


## GRIS, JUAN

Born José Victoriano Gonzales (later known as Juan Gris) in Madrid 23 March 1887. 1902 entered the Academy of Fine Arts in Madrid. After 1906 lived in Paris where he associated with Apollinaire, Picasso, Braque, Derain and Léger. Worked as illustrator to various periodicals before beginning to paint seriously in 1910. 1912 exhibited for the first time at the Salon des Indépendants and the "Section d'Or". 1913 spent some time in Céret with Picasso; 1914 met Matisse in Collioure. 1920 exhibited with the Cubists for the last time at an exhibition in the Salon des Indépendants. 1922—1923 designed ballet décors for Diaghilev. Died at Boulogne-sur-Seine 11 May 1927. Painted mostly still life, but also landscape and portraits: also numerous drawings, watercolours, gouaches, ballet décors and sculptures.

*Literature:* M. Raynal, Juan Gris, Paris 1920. — D. Henry, Juan Gris, Leipzig und Berlin 1929. — W. George, Juan Gris, Paris 1931. — D. H. Kahnweiler, Juan Gris, Sa vie, son œuvre, ses écrits, Paris 1946 (englische Ausgabe London und New York 1947). — D. Cooper, Juan Gris ou le Goût du Solennel, Genève 1949. — G. Schmidt, Juan Gris und die Geschichte des Kubismus, Baden-Baden 1957.


## HECKEL, ERICH

Born in Döbeln (Saxony) 31 July 1883. First studied architecture at the Dresden Technical School. Met Kirchner and Schmidt-Rottluff with whom in 1905 he founded the artists' group "Die Brücke", through which he learned lithography and wood-engraving, although he had taught himself painting. 1906 first exhibition of the group in Dresden. Military service in the medical corps in Flanders during the First World War. After the war he lived in Berlin with visits to South Germany, Italy and France. Denounced as degenerate by the Nazis. Since 1944 has lived in Hemmenhofen on Lake Constance. 1949 was appointed Professor at the Karlsruhe Academy.

*Literature:* L. Thormaehlen, Erich Heckel, Berlin 1930. — H. Köhn, Erich Heckel, Berlin 1948. — P. O. Rave, Erich Heckel, Berlin 1948.


## HODLER, FERDINAND

Born in Bern 14 March 1853. Received his first painting tuition from his stepfather, the decorative painter Schüpbach. 1867 went to Thun to work under the landscape painter Sommer. 1871 in Geneva, where he remained for the rest of his life except for brief visits to Basle 1875, Madrid 1878—1879 and Paris 1891. Pupil of Menn. 1887 first exhibition in Bern. 1890 painted the "Nacht" which established his fame. 1896 began his designs for the frescoes in the Swiss National Museum: "The Retreat from Marignano" which was to be of great significance in modern historical painting. 1904 exhibition at the Viennese Sezession. 1908 painted the "Exodus of the Jena students in 1813" at the Jena University. Many of his pictures are of allegorical scenes. Died in Geneva 20 May 1918.

*Literature:* F. Burger, Cézanne und Hodler. Einführung in die Probleme der Malerei der Gegenwart, 2 Bde., 2. Aufl., München 1918. — C. A. Loosli, Ferdinand Hodler. Mappenwerk, Zürich 1919. Leben, Werk und Nachlass, 4 Bde., Bern 1924. — Die Kunst Ferdinand Hodlers, Bd. I. Das Frühwerk bis 1895,

bearbeitet von E. Bender, Zürich 1923. Bd. II. Reife und Spätwerk, bearbeitet von W. Y. Müller, Zürich 1941. — D. Baud-Bovy, Les Hodler au Musée d'Art et d'Histoire de Genève, Genève 1940. — W. Hugelshofer, Ferdinand Hodler, Zürich 1952.


## JOHN, AUGUSTUS

Born in Tenby, Wales, 4 January 1878. 1894—1898 studied at the Slade School. 1901—1902 Professor of Painting at the Liverpool Art School. 1903 Member of the New English Art Club. Visited Wales and France accompanied by the painter Innes. Strongly influenced by the paintings of Rembrandt, Rubens, El Greco and the French 19th Century painters. 1942 was awarded the Order of Merit. John's works include mainly portraits, nudes, landscapes and flower-pieces.

*Literature:* J. Rothenstein, Augustus John, London 1944. — A. John, Chiaroscuro, Fragments of Autobiography, London 1952.


## JONES, DAVID

Born in Brockley, Kent, 1 November 1895. 1909 entered Camberwell School of Art. 1915—1918 military service. 1919 studied at the Westminster School of Art. 1925—1927 illustrations for the Golden Cockerell Press. 1927 returned to live at Brockley. First exhibition of paintings and drawings at St. George's Gallery. Member of the Society of Wood Engravers. 1929 an exhibition of his works at the Goupil Gallery included watercolours painted in France. 1930—1933 Member of the Seven and Five Society. 1933 works exhibited in Chicago; 1934 at the Venice Biennale; 1939 in New York. His principal writings are "In Parenthesis" 1937, and "The Anathemata: Fragments of an Attempted Writing" 1952. Painter, chiefly in watercolour, of portraits, animal, landscape and legendary, mythological and religious subjects; also woodengraver and designer of inscriptions.

*Literature:* R. Ironside, David Jones, London 1949.


## KANDINSKY, WASSILY

Born in Moscow 4 December 1866, where he studied law and economics. 1889 went to North East Russia with an expedition organized by the Moscow Association of Natural Science, Ethnology and Anthropology. 1896 gave up scientific work and went to Munich to study painting. Studied under Anton Azbe and later under Franz Stuck at the Academy. 1901 opened his own painting school and became President of the artists group "The Phalanx". Member of the Berlin Sezession. 1903—1908 visited Tunisia, Holland, Italy and France. From 1908 in Munich: founding of the new Munich Artists' Association. 1910 painted his first abstract picture and wrote his epoch-making work "Concerning the Spiritual in Art" which was published in Munich by Piper in 1912. 1911 founding of the "Blue Rider" group the most important members of which were Marc, Macke, Klee, Kubin and Campendonk. Exhibitions of the "Blue Rider" group at the Galleries Thannhauser and Goltz. 1914 visited Switzerland, and later returned to Russia. During the First World War he held important posts in Moscow and was also Professor at both the Academy and the University. 1921 in Germany again where in 1922 he was appointed Professor at the Bauhaus in Weimar; founded with Klee, Jawlensky and Feininger the "Blue Four" group. Moved to Dessau when the Bauhaus was transferred there. 1926 publication of his "From Point and Line to Plane". 1929 until 1931 visited Belgium, France, Egypt, Palestine, Syria, Turkey, Greece and Italy. 1933 denounced as decadent by the Nazis and went to live at Neuilly-sur-Seine, where he died 13 December 1944.

*Literature:* Kandinsky 1901—1913, Berlin 1913. — W. Grohmann, Wassily Kandinsky, Leipzig 1924. — W. Grohmann, Kandinsky, Paris 1930. — M. Arland, Kandinsky, Gouaches, Aquarelles, Dessins, Paris 1947. — C. Estienne, Kandinsky, Paris 1950. — M. Bill und andere, Wassily Kandinsky, Paris 1951. — W. Grohmann, Wassily Kandinsky. Leben und Werk, Köln 1958.

## KIRCHNER, ERNST LUDWIG

Born in Aschaffenburg 6 May 1880. 1901—1905 studied architecture in Dresden, with intermittent art and painting studies in Munich. 1905 in Dresden; founding of the artists' group "Die Brücke" to which at first Schmidt-Rottluff, Heckel and Bleyl also belonged, and later on, for a short time, Pechstein, Nolde and Müller. The first exhibition of the group in Dresden attracted scarcely any attention. 1907—1909 painted in the area around the Moritzburg Lake, near Dresden, with other members of the group. 1911 settled in Berlin. Became interested in the "Sturm". 1912 in conjunction with Heckel, painted frescoes for the International Sonderbund exhibition in Cologne. 1913 dissolution of the "Brücke". 1914 military service. After a physical and mental breakdown he spent some time in a Sanatorium in Taunus; 1917 convalescent in Kreuzlingen and Davos. Remained in Davos until his suicide 15 June 1938. Also graphic artist, sculptor and wood engraver.

*Literature:* G. Schiefler, Das graphische Werk Ernst Ludwig Kirchners, 2 Bde., Berlin 1920 und 1926. — W. Grohmann, Kirchners Zeichnungen, Dresden 1925. — W. Grohmann, Das Werk E. L. Kirchners, München 1926. — W. Grohmann, E. L. Kirchner, Stuttgart 1958.

## KLEE, PAUL

Born in Münchenbuchsee near Bern 18 December 1879. Studied painting under Knirr and later under Stuck at the Academy in Munich. 1901 visited Italy. 1903—1906 his earliest independent works included drawings and etchings, and later also watercolours. 1906 moved to Munich. Influenced by Cézanne, van Gogh and Marées. 1911 became acquainted with the painters of the "Blue Rider" group. 1912 exhibited at the second exhibition of the "Blue Rider" group in Munich. Visited Paris where he met Picasso and Delaunay. Strongly influenced by Cubism. 1914 visited Tunisia and Kairouan with Macke and Moillet. Military service in Germany during the First World War. 1920 exhibition at the Galerie Goltz in Munich; joined the staff of the Bauhaus in Weimar. 1925 exhibited at the first Surrealist exhibition in Paris. Member of the "Blue Four" artists' group. 1931 appointed Professor at the Düsseldorf Academy. 1933 returned to Switzerland where he remained until his death on 29 June 1940.

*Literature:* H. F. Geist, Paul Klee, Hamburg 1948. — D. H. Kahnweiler, Klee, Paris, New York 1950. — W. Haftmann, Paul Klee. Wege bildnerischen Denkens, München 1950. — C. Giedion-Welcker, Paul Klee, New York 1952. — A. Forge, Paul Klee, London 1954. — W. Grohmann, Paul Klee, Stuttgart 1954. — Paul Klee, Das bildnerische Denken, nachgelassene Schriften zur Form- und Gestaltungslehre, hg. von Jürg Spiller, Basel-Stuttgart 1956. — N. Hulton, An Approach to Paul Klee, London 1956. — W. Mehring, Klee, Bern 1956.

## KOKOSCHKA, OSKAR

Born in Pöchlarn (Danube) 1 March 1886. 1904—1908 studied at the Vienna School of Arts and Crafts. Influenced by Klimt. 1908 his works were exhibited for the first time in Vienna. 1909 went to Switzerland; 1910 to Berlin where he founded the "Sturm". 1916 wounded on the East Front during the First World War. 1918—1924 in Dresden where in 1920 he became a teacher at the Academy of Fine Arts. 1924 gave up teaching. Travelled extensively in Europe and the Mediterranean countries. 1931 in Vienna from where he emigrated to Prague in 1934 after the assassination of Dollfuss. 1938 fled to London on the invasion of Czechoslovakia by the Nazis. After the Second World War he visited America, Germany and Venice. 1953 settled in Villeneuve on Lake Geneva.

*Literature:* P. Westheim, Oskar Kokoschka, 2. Aufl. Berlin 1925. — G. Biermann, Oskar Kokoschka, Leipzig 1929. — H. Heilmaier, Kokoschka, Paris 1929. — E. Hoffmann, Oskar Kokoschka. Life and work, London 1947. — H. M. Wingler, Oskar Kokoschka. Das Werk des Malers, Salzburg 1956. — B. Bultmann, Oskar Kokoschka, Salzburg 1959.

## LEGER, FERNAND

Born in Argentan (Normandy) 4 February 1881. Began his career as an architectural draughtsman. 1902—1905 pupil of Gérôme, and later of Ferrier at the Ecole des Beaux-Arts in Paris. Was influenced first by the Neo-Impressionists and later by Cézanne and the Fauves. 1909 joined Apollinaire's circle and the Cubists. 1910 exhibited for the first time at the Salon des Indépendants. During his military service in the First World War he drew soldiers and war machines. 1916 suffered gas poisoning in Verdun and was subsequently discharged. Period of pictures of mechanical and dynamic content. After 1921 the human form assumed greater significance in Léger's painting. 1921—1924 décors for ballet. Co-operated in the film "Ballet Mécanique". 1924 visited Ravenna and Venice. Became associated with the painters of the "Stijl". 1931 first visit to America. 1937 frescoes for the Palace of Discovery at the Paris World's Fair. 1938 second visit to America. 1940—1945 lived in America. In his later years turned to handicraft work and designed mosaics for the façade of the church at Assy, and stained-glass windows for the church at Audincourt. Also potteries and some sculpture. Died 17 August 1955.

*Literature:* D. Cooper, Fernand Léger et le nouvel espace, Genève 1949. — K. Kuh, Léger, Urbana (USA) 1953. — A. Verdet, Fernand Léger, Genève 1955.

## LEWIS, WYNDHAM

Born in Nova Scotia or the USA 1882 or December 1884, of British parents. 1898—1901 studied at the Slade School. 1902—1908 worked in Paris, Germany, Holland and Spain, and finally returned to England. 1911 Member of the Camden Town Group. 1912 exhibited at the second Post-Impressionist exhibition at the Grafton Galleries. 1913 Member of the London Group. Extensive writings on art and other subjects after 1914. Founded the Vorticist Group and edited its paper "Blast". During the First World War he served with the Artillery and later as Official War Artist to the Canadian Corps Headquarters. 1919 an exhibition was held at the Goupil Gallery of his pictures of war subjects. 1921—1922 edited the art review "The Tyro" and 1927—1929 "The Enemy". 1940—1948 in Canada and America. 1949 retrospective exhibition the Redfern Gallery, and 1956 at the Tate Gallery. Died in London 7 February 1957.

*Literature:* H. G. Porteous, Wyndham Lewis, London 1932. — W. Lewis, Wyndham Lewis the Artist, from Blast to Burlington House, London 1939. — Ch. Handley-Read (ed.), The Art of Wyndham Lewis, London 1951.

## MACKE, AUGUST

Born in Meschede (Ruhr) 3 January 1887. 1904—1906 studied at the Düsseldorf Academy. Visited Italy, Holland, Belgium, London and Paris. 1907 studied under Lovis Corinth in Berlin. Further visits to Paris brought him into contact with the Impressionists, the Fauves and the Cubists. 1910 met Marc in Tegernsee and joined the new Munich Artists' Association. 1912 exhibited at the exhibition of the "Blue Rider" group. In Paris with Marc in the Autumn, where he met Delaunay. 1913—1914 lived near the Thunersee with the Swiss painter Moilliet. 1914 visited Kairuan in Tunisia, with Klee and Moilliet. Died in action in Champagne 26 September 1914.

*Literature:* W. Cohen, August Macke, Leipzig 1922. — G. Vriesen, August Macke, Stuttgart 1953.

## MARC, FRANZ

Born in Munich 8 February 1880. 1900—1902 studied at the Munich Academy. Visited Italy and France where he came into contact with the Impressionists. 1907 in Paris where he was greatly impressed by the works of van Gogh. Painted in the Berlin Zoo. Spent the Summer months in quiet meadows where he studied animals. 1910 met Macke and Kandinsky. 1911 exhibited at the first exhibition of the "Blue Rider" group of which he was a joint-founder. 1912 edited the "Blue Rider" publication in conjunction with Kandinsky. The works of Delaunay, whom Marc met in Paris in the autumn, made a great impression on him. 1914 volunteered for military service; died in action at Verdun 4 March 1916. Painter, graphic artist, sculptor and writer.

*Literature:* Franz Marc, Briefe, Aufzeichnungen und Aphorismen, 2 Bde., Berlin 1920. — A. J. Schardt, Franz Marc, Berlin 1936. — K. Lankheit, Franz Marc, Berlin 1950. — H. Bünemann, Franz Marc, Zeichnungen — Aquarelle, 2. Aufl. München 1952.


MARIN, JOHN

Born in Rutherford, New Jersey, 23 December 1870. First studied architecture, and in 1893 opened his own Architect's Office. 1899 studied painting at the Philadelphia Art Academy and joined the Art Students' League. 1905 until 1910 lived in Paris during which time he worked in various studios and academies. 1910 exhibition of watercolours at the Stieglitz Gallery in New York and at the Salon d'Automne in Paris. Visited Austria and later returned to America. 1929—1930 lived in Mexico. 1936 big exhibition of his work held at the Museum of Modern Art, New York, and in 1950 at the Venice Biennale. Died 1953. Marin is recognized as one of the pioneers of avantgarde painting in America, having created a form of art free from academic influences.

*Literature:* E. M. Benson, John Marin, the Man and his Work, Washington 1935. — R. Flint, John Marin, New York n. d. — M. Helm, John Marin, Boston 1948.


MARQUET, ALBERT

Born in Bordeaux 27 March 1875. 1890 entered the School of Arts and Crafts in Paris. Friendly with Matisse. 1897 entered the Ecole des Beaux-Arts where he was a pupil of Gustave Moreau. Joined the Fauve movement and from 1901 until 1910 exhibited at their exhibitions at the Salon des Indépendants. After 1908 travelled extensively in Europe and North Africa. 1913 with Matisse in Morocco, later settling, near Matisse, in Marseilles and Nice. 1928 visited Egypt and Assuan; 1934 visited Russia. 1936—1937 lived in Switzerland and 1940—1945 in Algeria. 1945 returned to Paris, where he died 14 June 1947.

*Literature:* F. Fosca, Albert Marquet, Paris 1922. — G. Besson, Marquet, Genève 1948. — M. Marquet et F. Daulte, Marquet, Lausanne 1953. — M. Marquet, Marquet, Paris 1955.


MATISSE, HENRI

Born at Le Cateau, France, 31 December 1869. At his father's wish he began to study law which did not, however, appeal to him. Began to paint in secret, and in 1891 obtained his parents' permission to take painting lessons. 1892 entered Julian's. The following year he became a pupil of Gustave Moreau at the Ecole des Beaux-Arts. 1896—1898 visited Belle Isle, Corsica and Toulouse. Adopted the Impressionist style of painting and was later much influenced by Cézanne. After 1903 exhibited regularly at the Salon d'Automne. 1904 first one-man exhibition at Vollard's. 1905 exhibited at the Salon d'Automne together with Derain, Vlaminck, Rouault and Manguin: became the leader of the Fauve group. Became acquainted with Picasso. Founded his own art school which soon closed down however. 1908—1913 visited Germany, Spain, Russia and Morocco. 1917 settled in Nice: period of the odalisks. 1930—1931 visited America and Tahiti. 1931—1933 engaged on the "Dance" for the Barnes Foundation. 1932 illustrations for Mallarmé's "Poesies". 1949 until 1951 last great work — the chapel at Vence. Died in Nice 3 November 1954. Painter, illustrator, graphic artist and sculptor.

*Literature:* E. Faure, J. Romain, Ch. Vildrac et L. Werth, Henri Matisse, Paris 1921. — G. Jedlicka, Henri Matisse, Paris 1930. — A. Barnes and V. de

Mazia, The art of Henri Matisse, New York 1933. — P. Courthion, Henri Matisse, Paris 1934. — R. Escholier, Henri Matisse, Paris 1937. — G. Besson, Matisse, Paris 1943. — I. Grunewald, Matisse och expressionismen, Stockholm 1944. — A. H. J. Barr, Matisse, his Art and his Public, New York 1951. — G. Diehl, Henri Matisse, Paris 1954. — R. Escholier, Matisse ce vivent, Paris 1956. — J. Lassaigne, Matisse, Genève 1959.


MIRO, JOAN

Born in Montroig, near Barcelona, 20 April 1893. 1907 entered the Art Academy in Barcelona. His first paintings, which he exhibited in 1918, show the influence of van Gogh and the Fauves. 1919 visited Paris where he came under the influence of Picasso. 1925 exhibited at the first Surrealist exhibition at the Galerie Pierre in Paris. Worked with Max Ernst on the décors and costumes for Diaghilev's Russian Ballet. Strongly influenced by Klee. 1928 visited Holland. 1931—1932 designed the décors and costumes for the ballet "Jeux d'Enfants" for the Monte Carlo Ballet. 1937 painted the fresco for the Spanish Pavilion at the Paris World's Fair. 1940 returned to Barcelona where he began to paint ceramics. 1947 visited America. Painted the fresco in the Hotel Plaza at Cincinnati. Since 1948 has lived in Barcelona, with frequent visits to Paris.

*Literature:* J. J. Sweeney, Joan Miró, New York 1941. — C. Greenberg, Joan Miró, New York 1948. — A. Cirici-Pellicer, Miró y la Imaginacion, Barcelona 1949. — J. E. Cirlot, Joan Miró, Barcelona 1949. — E. Hüttinger, Joan Miró, Bern 1957. — J. Th. Soby, Joan Miró, New York 1959.


MODERSOHN-BECKER, PAULA

Born in Dresden 8 February 1876. 1888 moved to Bremen. 1892 spent some time in London where she received her first instruction in drawing. Lived, from 1897, in Worpswede, the centre of paintings of North German peasant life. Studied under Mackensen. 1900 first visit to Paris where she entered the Colarossi Academy. 1901 married the painter Otto Modersohn. Visited Prague and Munich, and later returned to Worpswede. Visited Paris 1903, 1905 and 1906—1907. Died in Worpswede 30 November 1907.

*Literature:* Paula Modersohn-Becker, Briefe und Tagebuchblätter, München 1920. — G. Pauli, Paula Modersohn-Becker, 2. Aufl. München 1922. — G. Biermann, Paula Modersohn, Leipzig und Berlin 1927. — R. Hetsch, Paula Modersohn-Becker, Berlin 1932. — M. Hausmann, Paula Modersohn-Becker, Biberach 1947.


MODIGLIANI, AMEDEO

Born in Leghorn 12 July 1884. Had his first painting lessons at the age of 14 from a landscape painter in Leghorn. 1900 studied painting in the museums at Rome, Venice and Florence. 1906 in Paris. 1908 exhibited for the first time at the Salon des Indépendants. 1909 in Italy. Became friendly with Brancusi. The Cézanne exhibition at Bernheim-Jeune in 1910 made a great impression on him. After 1913 lived in Montparnasse. 1918 the first collective exhibition at Berthe Weill was closed by the police after a few days. Winter 1918—1919 in Nice and Cagnes on account of poor health. Died of tuberculosis in Paris 25 January 1920.

*Literature:* A. Salmon, Modigliani, sa vie et son œuvre, Paris 1926. — G. Scheiwiller, Amedeo Modigliani, Milano 1927. — A. Pfannstiel, Modigliani, Paris 1929. — R. Franchi, Modigliani, Firenze 1946. — P. Descargues, Amedeo Modigliani, Paris 1951. — J. Th. Soby, Modigliani. Paintings, Drawings, Sculpture, New York 1951. — E. Carli, Amedeo Modigliani, Roma 1952. — G. Jedlicka, Modigliani, Erlenbach-Zürich 1953. — A. Pfannstiel, Modigliani et son œuvre, Paris 1956. — C. Roy, Modigliani, Genève 1958. — A. Salmon, Amedeo Modigliani, Zürich 1960.

## MONDRIAN, PIET

Born in Amersfoort, Holland, 7 March 1872. His first attempts at painting were made under the guidance of his uncle Frits Mondrian. 1892—1894 studied at the Imperial Academy in Amsterdam. Until 1910 painted still life and naturalistic landscapes in various parts of Holland. 1908 under the influence of Matisse he began to use clear colours. 1910 first stay in Paris where he came under the influence of Cubism. 1914 returned to Holland and began to paint abstract pictures consisting of vertical and horizontal lines. 1917 founded the journal "De Stijl" with Theo van Doesburg. In Paris again after the First World War. 1920 "Le Neo-Plasticisme" published, in which he set out his theory of abstract painting. 1938 moved to London; 1940 to New York where he died 1 February 1944.

*Literature:* J. J. Sweeney, Mondrian, New York 1948. M. Seuphor, Mondrian, Stuttgart 1956.


## MOORE, HENRY

Born in Castleford, Yorkshire, 30 July 1898, the seventh child of a miner. 1917—1919 military service. 1919—1921 studied at the Leeds School of Art. 1921—1924 at the Royal College of Art, where he won a travelling scholarship which took him, in 1924, to France and Italy. 1924—1939 taught at the Royal College of Art and later at the Chelsea School of Art. 1928 first one-man exhibition at the Warren Gallery, followed in successive years by exhibitions in Venice, Berlin, Stockholm, Zürich and Hamburg. 1930—1937 Member of the London Group. Exhibited at the International Surrealist exhibition in London 1936, and in Paris 1938. 1937 visited Spain; 1946 New York; 1951 Greece; and Paris and Italy on several occasions. After the Second World War exhibitions of his work were shown in many cities in Europe, North and South America, Australia and Africa. Member of various art commissions, received numerous awards and the Honorary Doctorate of the Universities of Leeds and London. Drawings and sketches, in addition to sculpture, form an important part of his work as a whole.

*Literature:* G. Grigson, Henry Moore, London 1943. — Henry Moore: Sculpture and Drawings, with an Introduction by Herbert Read, London 1944. Vol. II, Sculpture and Drawings since 1948, London 1955.


## MUNCH, EDVARD

Born in Loeiten, Norway, 12 December 1863. The deaths at an early age of his mother and sister Sophie were significant events in his youth which may be traced throughout his works. 1881—1884 studied painting in Oslo. 1885 visited Paris for the first time. After being awarded a State scholarship he spent the winter of 1889 in Paris again. Particularly impressed by the paintings of the Neo-Impressionists, of Toulouse-Lautrec, van Gogh and Gauguin. Visited Germany for the first time. 1891 visited France and Italy. 1892 an exhibition at the Berlin Artists' Association was closed after a very short time. 1895 co-operated in the designs for "Pan". His first lithographs were shown in Paris. 1896 first wood engravings. Decorations for "Peer Gynt" at the Théâtre de l'Oeuvre. 1897 exhibition of the "Frieze of Life" at the Salon des Indépendants. 1898—1901 visited Germany on several occasions. 1902 friendly with Dr. Max Linde in Lübeck for whom he painted a second "Frieze of Life". 1906 a third "Frieze of Life" was commissioned by Reinhardt for the foyer of the Kammerspiele in Berlin. 1908—1909 spent some time in Copenhagen at the Jacobsen Clinic for Nervous Diseases. 1909—1915 worked intermittently on the murals for the Assembly Hall of the University of Oslo. 1920—1922 visited Berlin, Paris and Italy. 1922 important exhibition in Zürich. 1937 exhibition at the Norwegian Pavilion at the Paris World's Fair. Died at his estate in Ekely 23 January 1944.

*Literature:* C. Glaser, Edvard Munch, Berlin 1917 (2. Aufl. 1922). — J. P. Hodin, Edvard Munch, Stockholm 1948. — R. Stenersen, Edvard Munch, Zürich 1949. — O. Benesch, Edvard Munch, London 1960.


## NASH, PAUL

Born in Kensington, London, 11 May 1889. 1901—1906 attended St. Paul's School and later the Slade School. 1912 first exhibition of drawings and water-colours at the Carfax Gallery. 1917 invalided out of the army. Appointed Official War Artist as a result of his exhibition "Ypres Salient". 1919 Member of the New English Art Club; 1922 Member of the Association of Wood-Engravers. 1921—1925 lived in Dymchurch, Kent. 1922 visited Paris for the first time. 1924—1925 taught drawing at the Royal College of Art. 1929—1930 in France again. 1926, 1932 and 1938 exhibitions at the Venice Biennale. 1933 until 1934 visited France, Spain and North Africa. 1936 returned to London. Exhibited at the Surrealist exhibition in London, and in 1938 in Paris. Official War Artist again in the Second World War. Retrospective exhibition in Leeds 1943 and in Cheltenham 1945. Died in Boscombe, Hants, 11 July 1946. Landscape, nude and still life painter and wood engraver. Influenced at first by Cézanne and later turned to Surrealism and Constructivism.

*Literature:* H. Read, Paul Nash, London 1944. — M. Eates (ed.), Paul Nash, Paintings, Drawings and Illustrations, London 1948. — P. Nash, Outline, an Autobiography and other Writings, London 1949. — A. Bertram, Paul Nash, the Portrait of an Artist, London 1955.


## NICHOLSON, BEN

Born in Denham, Bucks., 10 April 1894. 1910—1911 studied painting at the Slade School in London; later in Tours and Milan. 1913—1914 in Madeira. 1914—1917 in London and Wales. 1917—1918 in Pasadena (California); 1920 until 1931 in Castagnola (Switzerland), Cumberland and London. 1925—1936 Member of the Seven and Five Society. 1933 exhibited at an exhibition in Paris of works by the "Abstraction-Creation" group. Exhibitions in Venice, Brussels, Lucerne, Amsterdam and New York. 1944 retrospective exhibition in Leeds. 1954 awarded the "Ulissi" Prize at the Venice Biennale. Has lived, since 1940, at St. Ives, Cornwall. Was the first important exponent of abstract painting in England. During the last 30 years he has painted very stylised still life and landscape, also abstract compositions, sometimes in low relief.

*Literature:* J. Summerson, Ben Nicholson, London 1948. — H. Read (ed.), Ben Nicholson, Paintings, Reliefs, Drawings, London 1948. — H. Read (ed.), Ben Nicholson, work since 1941, Vol. II, London 1956.


## NOLDE, EMIL

Born, Emil Hansen, in Nolde (North Schleswig) 7 August 1867. 1884—1888 attended the Sauermann School of Wood Engraving in Flensburg. Worked as a wood sculptor in Munich and Karlsruhe. 1892—1898 taught at the School of Arts and Crafts at St. Gallen; afterwards worked as a free-lance painter and sculptor. Studied in Munich, Paris and Copenhagen. 1906 exhibited at the exhibitions of the German Artists' Federation and the Berlin "Sezession". 1907 Member of the "Brücke" in Dresden for a short time. 1910 in Hamburg. 1911 visited Belgium and Holland. 1913 member of a scientific expedition to the Pacific, via Russia, China and Japan. During the First World War worked mainly in Berlin and Alsen. 1927 Jubilee exhibition in Dresden. 1931 publication of his autobiography "Das eigene Leben" and three years later the sequel "Jahre der Kämpfe". 1937 works confiscated by the Nazis as decadent. 1946 designated Professor by the Schleswig-Holstein authorities. Died at his Estate in Seebüll 15 April 1956.

*Literature:* M. Sauerlandt, Emil Nolde, München 1922. — P. F. Schmidt, Emil Nolde, Leipzig 1929. — M. Gosebruch, Emil Nolde, Aquarelle und Zeichnungen, München 1957. — Katalog der Gedächtnisausstellung Emil Nolde, Kunstverein in Hamburg 1957.


## PECHSTEIN, MAX

Born in Zwickau 31 December 1881. Studied at the School of Arts and Crafts and later at the Art Academy in Dresden. 1906 met Heckel and Kirchner.

Joined the "Brücke" group. 1907 in Italy. From 1908 in Berlin and East Prussia. 1914 visited the South Sea Island of Palau. 1922 Member of the Prussian Academy of Fine Arts, from which he was dimissed in 1933. 1924—1925 in Switzerland and Italy; 1931 in the South of France. Died in Berlin 1955. Painter, glass painter, graphic artist and sculptor.

*Literature:* W. Heymann, Max Pechstein, München 1916. — G. Biermann, Max Pechstein, Leipzig 1919. — M. Osborn, Max Pechstein, Berlin 1922.


## PICASSO, PABLO

Born in Malaga 25 October 1881. 1891 moved with his family to La Coruña in Galicia. Received his first painting lessons from his father who taught at the School of Arts and Crafts. 1895 continued his studies in Barcelona. At the age of 15 opened his own studio in Barcelona, and held his first exhibition there in 1897. Worked as an illustrator for periodicals. 1900 visited Paris for the first time. 1901 founded the art magazine "Arte Joven" in Madrid, which he himself illustrated. Second visit to Paris; exhibited at Vollard's and became associated with Max Jacob. Beginning of the Blue Period. 1904—1909 in Paris. Became acquainted with Apollinaire, Matisse, Braque, Derain and Kahnweiler. 1905 beginning of the Pink Period. 1906—1907 painted "Les Demoiselles d'Avignon". 1907 Negro Period. 1908 the paintings of this period show the influence of Cézanne. 1909 in Horta de Ebro. First exhibition in Germany at the Galerie Thannhauser in Munich. Beginning of a period of analytical Cubism. In the summer of 1910 worked with Derain in Cadaqués, and in the following two years with Braque in Céret. 1912 beginning of period of synthetic Cubism. 1913 in Céret again with Braque and Juan Gris. In Paris from the outbreak of war. 1917 with Jean Cocteau in Rome. Designs for the décors and costumes for Diaghilev's Russian Ballet. Until 1924 he undertook many commissions for ballet décors. 1925 exhibited at the first Surrealist exhibition in Paris. After 1928 repeatedly turned to plastic arts. 1931 Illustrations for Ovid's "Metamorphoses". 1934 spent some time in Spain. 1936 travelling exhibition of his works shown in Barcelona, Bilbao and Madrid. Became Director of the Prado. 1937 painted the very large work "Guernica" for the Spanish Pavilion at the Paris World's Fair. During the Second World War worked mostly around Bordeaux and in Paris. After the liberation of Paris he exhibited for the first time at the Salon d'Automne. 1947 in Vallauris: revival of ceramic art. 1949 visited Italy. Etchings for Prosper Mérimée's "Carmen". 1953 important retrospective exhibition in Rome, Milan, Lyons and Sao Paolo. Lives at present in Vallauris.

*Literature:* M. Raynal, Picasso, München 1921. W. Uhde, Picasso et la tradition française, Paris 1928. — G. Stein, Picasso, Paris 1938. — J. Cassou, Picasso, Paris 1940 (nouv. éd. 1946). — A. H. Barr, Picasso. Fifty Years of his Art, New York 1946. — M. Raynal, Picasso (deutsche Übersetzung von K. G. Hemmerich), Genf 1953. — J. Sabartés, Picasso. Documents iconographiques, Genève 1954. — W. Boeck, Pablo Picasso, Stuttgart 1955. — R. Penrose, Picasso, his life and work, London 1958.


## RIVERA, DIEGO

Born in Guanajuato, Mexico, 8 December 1886. First painting lessons in Mexico City at the age of 12. 1907 awarded a painting scholarship in Europe. First spent two years in Madrid where he studied Spanish painting; later moved to Paris where he was strongly influenced by Picasso, Braque and Gris. After spending several years in Paris he went to Munich, thence to Italy and finally to Russia. 1921 returned to Mexico: revival of Mayan and Aztec art. Important commissions for mural paintings in public buildings in Mexico and America. His main themes are history and Mexican social and political life.

*Literature:* E. Edwards, Frescoes by Diego Rivera in Cuernavaca, Mexico 1933. — Diego Rivera, 50 annos de su labor artistica, Mexico 1951.


## ROUAULT, GEORGES

Born in Paris 27 May 1871. At the age of 14 began his training as a glass painter and restored old stained-glass windows. 1891 entered the Ecole des Beaux-Arts where he was a pupil of Gustave Moreau. Met Matisse. 1903 met Huysmans and became friendly with Léon Bloy. Exhibited at the first Salon d'Automne with Matisse and Marquet. Was for a time a member of the Fauve group. 1916 came to an agreement with Vollard who had exclusive rights over his works. Commissions for series of graphic works: "Les Réincarnations du Père Ubu", "Le Cirque", "Les Fleurs du Mal", "Miserere et Guerre". 1929 décors for Diaghilev's ballet "L'Enfant prodigue". Since 1940 has painted almost exclusively religious subjects. 1948 law-suit with Vollard's successors. Rouault burned 315 pictures. Visited Italy and executed stained-glass windows for the church at Assy in Haute Savoie. 1949 visited Belgium and Holland. Died in Paris 13 February 1958.

*Literature:* M. Puy, Georges Rouault, Paris 1921. — B. Charensol, Georges Rouault. L'homme et l'œuvre, Paris 1926. — L. Venturi, Georges Rouault, New York 1940 (nouv. éd. Paris 1948). — B. Dorival, Rouault, Paris 1942. — M. Brion, Georges Rouault, Paris 1950. — M. Morel, Le Miserere de Georges Rouault, Paris 1951. — B. Derival, Georges Rouault, Genève 1956. — L. Venturi, Georges Rouault, Genève 1959.


## SCHLEMMER, OSKAR

Born in Stuttgart 4 September 1888. Studied at the School of Arts and Crafts and at the Stuttgart Academy under A. Hölzel. Volunteered for military service during the First World War. 1929—1929 taught at the Bauhaus in Weimar, and later in Dessau. 1929—1931 Professor at the Breslau Academy and later in Berlin. 1933 dismissed from State service. Lived until 1937 in Eichberg (Baden) and from 1937 until his death, in Sehringen near Badenweiler. Died in Baden-Baden 13 April 1943.

*Literature:* G. Schmidt, Oskar Schlemmer, Bern-Bümpliz 1949. — H. Hildebrandt, Oskar Schlemmer, München 1952.


## SCHMIDT-ROTTLUFF, KARL

Born in Rottluff, near Chemnitz, 1 December 1884. At first studied architecture in Dresden, where he met Heckel and Kirchner and with them founded in 1906 the "Brücke" which Pechstein, Nolde and others joined later. Spent some time on the Island of Alsen. 1911 in Norway and later in Berlin where he contributed to the journal "Der Sturm". Met Otto Müller and Feininger. 1912 exhibited at the "Sonderbund" exhibition in Cologne and at the exhibition of the "Blue Rider" group in Munich. 1913 dissolution of the "Brücke". At the Russian Front during the First World War. 1924 visited Paris with the sculptor Kolbe. 1930 long stay in Rome. 1931 appointed Member of the Prussian Academy in Berlin. 1933 dismissed from the Academy by the Nazis. 1937 608 of his works confiscated by the Nazis as degenerate. 1941 forbidden to paint. After the Second World War he was appointed Professor at the Berlin Academy.

*Literature:* W. Valentiner, Karl Schmidt-Rottluff, Leipzig 1920. — W. Grohmann, Karl Schmidt-Rottluff, Stuttgart 1956.


## SEVERINI, GINO

Born in Corona 7 April 1883. 1901 went to Rome where he met Boccioni and Balla. 1906 moved to Paris where he met Picasso, Max Jacob, Apollinaire and Braque. 1910 signed, with Carrà, Boccioni, Russolo, Marinetti and Balla, the Manifesto of Futurist Painting. 1912 exhibited at the first Futurist exhibition at Bernheim-Jeune in Paris. After 1915 his style gradually became more Neoclassic; since the 1940's has reverted to decorative Cubism. In recent years his works show the strong influence of concrete art. 1950 awarded a Biennale Prize.

*Literature:* J. Maritain, Gino Severini, Paris 1930. — J. Cassou, Gino Severini, Paris 1933. — P. Courthion, Cino Severini, Milano 1941.

## SMITH, MATTHEW

Born in Halifax 22 October 1879, the son of a wire manufacturer. Worked for four years in his father's factory before entering the Manchester School of Art to study design. 1905—1907 studied at the Slade School in London. 1910 in Paris where he attended the short-lived school run by Matisse. Until 1939 lived alternately in France and England. First exhibition at Tooth's London 1926. Retrospective exhibitions of his work held at the Venice Biennale 1938 and 1950, and in Leeds 1942. Nudes, still life and landscape are his main themes.

*Literature:* Ph. Hendy, Matthew Smith, London 1944.

## SPENCER, STANLEY

Born in Cookham, Berks., 30 June 1891. 1907 entered the Maidenhead Technical Institute. 1908—1912 studied at the Slade School. 1912 exhibited at the second Post-Impressionist exhibition in London. Served in the Royal Army Medical Corps during the First World War. 1919—1927 Member of the New English Art Club. 1922 visited Jugoslavia. 1926—1932 wall paintings, The Oratory of All Souls, Burghclere. 1927 exhibition at the Goupil Gallery. 1940 commissioned by the War Artists Advisory Committee to paint pictures of shipyards in Glasgow. 1953 visited China as a member of a cultural delegation. 1955 retrospective exhibition of his paintings held at the Tate Gallery. Paints mainly religious subjects, also landscape and portraits.

*Literature:* R. H. Wilenski, Stanley Spencer, London 1924. — E. Rothenstein, Stanley Spencer, London 1945. — S. Spencer, Introduction to the Catalogue of the Spencer Retrospective Exhibition, London 1955.

## SOUTINE, CHAIM

Born in Smilovitch, near Minsk, 1894, of a poor Jewish family. Left home at an early age and moved first to Minsk and in 1910 to Wilna, where he entered the Academy. Worked for a time as an assistant to a photographer. 1911 the assistance of a friend made it possible for him to move to Paris where he studied painting under Cormon at the Ecole des Beaux-Arts. Met Chagall, Laurens, Lipchitz and Léger. Friendly with Modigliani who introduced him to the dealer Zborowski. 1919 on the advice of Zborowski moved to Céret in the South of France, and returned in 1922 with over 200 pictures. Spent some time in Cannes. From 1929 lived near Chartres. Died in Paris 9 August 1943.

*Literature:* E. Faure, Soutine, Paris 1928. — R. Cogniat, Soutine, Paris 1945. — M. Wheeler, Chaïm Soutine, New York 1950.

## SUTHERLAND, GRAHAM

Born in London 24 August 1903. 1919 entered Goldsmiths College of Art. Worked at first mainly as etcher and illustrator. 1925 first exhibition of his drawings and etchings in London. From 1930 taught at the Chelsea School of Art. Distinct changes visible in his style after he spent some time in Pembrokeshire in 1936. Discovered a new life within the plant and mineral world which had considerable influence on his painting. 1938 first exhibition of his painting in London. 1940—1944 Official War Artist. 1946 painted a large Crucifixion in St. Matthew's Church in Northampton. Retrospective exhibitions in London 1951; in Venice and Paris 1952. 1952 commissioned to design tapestries for the new Coventry Cathedral. 1953 big exhibition at the Tate Gallery, which was later shown in Amsterdam, Zürich and Boston.

*Literature:* E. Sackville-West, Graham Sutherland, London 1943 (revised edition 1955). — R. Melville, Graham Sutherland, London 1950.

## TANGUY, YVES

Born in Paris 5 January 1900, of Breton parents. Served for a time in the Merchant Navy. Visited England, Spain, Portugal and South America. 1924 much impressed by a picture by de Chirico which he had seen on display at the Galerie Guillaume in Paris, he began to paint, without instruction. 1925 joined the Surrealists and exhibited at their exhibitions from 1927. 1939 went to live in America. Died in Woodbury (Connecticut) 1955.

*Literature:* R. Renne and C. Serbanne, Yves Tanguy or the mirror of wonders, New York 1945. — A. Breton, Yves Tanguy, New York 1946.

## TOULOUSE-LAUTREC, HENRI DE

Born in Albi 24 November 1864, the son of Count Alphonse de Toulouse-Lautrec. 1869 moved to Paris with his mother who was supervising his education. 1878 and 1879 sustained two leg fractures which healed badly and left him a cripple. Decided to become a painter and was given his first drawing instruction by the animal painter Princeteau. Later worked for some time in the studios of Bonnard and Cormon. Taught himself decorative painting in which he was influenced by Degas and by Japanese wood engravings. 1885 moved to his own studio in Montmartre. Mixed exclusively in Bohemian circles and worked in places of entertainment, in cabarets and brothels whose penetrating and indefatigable chronicler he became. 1891—1892 designed his first posters and coloured lithographs. Contributed to the "Revue Blanche". 1895 visited London where he met Wilde. 1897 alcohol and excessive night-life began to undermine his weak constitution. 1899 entered St. James's Sanatorium at Neuilly. Died at his mother's castle at Malromé 9 September 1901.

*Literature:* L. Delteil, Henri de Toulouse-Lautrec, Paris 1920 (Vol. X, XI of "Le peintre-graveur illustré"). — Th. Duret, Lautrec, Paris 1920. — G. Jedlicka, Toulouse-Lautrec, Berlin 1929 und Erlenbach-Zürich 1943. — J. Lassaigne, Toulouse-Lautrec, Genève 1953. — D. Cooper, Henri de Toulouse-Lautrec, Stuttgart und Zürich 1955.

## UTRILLO, MAURICE

Born in Paris 26 December 1883, the son of the painter Suzanne Valadon. 1891 was adopted by the Spanish art critic Miguel Utrillo. In his school-days he already drank excessively. Worked for a time in a bank from which he was soon dismissed. First stay in an institute for alcoholics. 1902 encouraged by his mother, he began to paint. Painted his first landscape of Montmagny and Montmartre in dark colours with heavy brush-strokes, later coming under the influence of the Impressionists, particularly Pissarro. 1908—1910 painted the Cathedrals of Paris, Reims and Rouen. 1912 visited Brittany; 1913 Corsica. His work as a painter was frequently interrupted by periods spent in institutes for alcoholics. 1908—1914 the "White Period" during which his best works were painted. 1923 an exhibition was held at Bernheim-Jeune which laid the foundations of his success. 1924 settled with his mother and the painter Utter in a villa in Montmartre. Period of brightly coloured pictures. In his last years he led a more civilized life, marked by a distinct diminishing of his inspiration and artistic powers. Died 5 November 1955.

*Literature:* F. Carco, Maurice Utrillo, Paris 1921. — G. Coquiot, Maurice Utrillo, Paris 1925. — A. Tabarant, Utrillo, Paris 1926. — F. Carco, La légende et la vie d'Utrillo, Paris 1928. — A. Basler, Maurice Utrillo, Paris 1931. — P. Courthion, Utrillo, Bern 1947. — J. Jourdain, Maurice Utrillo, Paris 1948. — P. Mac Orlan, Utrillo, Paris 1952. — P. Pétridès, L'œuvre complet de Maurice Utrillo. Vol I. 1904—1914, Paris 1959.

## VAN GOGH, VINCENT

Born in Groot-Zundert, Holland, 30 March 1853, the eldest son of a Protestant clergyman. 1869 apprenticed to the art dealer Goupil in the Hague. At the age of 20 he was sent to their London branch. Later, in Paris, he became very interested in the study of the Bible and religion. 1876 returned to England where for a time he taught French in Ramsgate. After being dismissed he worked as an evangelist with a Methodist preacher. 1877 began to study theology and went as a missionary to the mining district of Borinage. First attempts at painting: returned to his parents' house in Etten. Decided to take up painting as a career and studied under Mauve at the Hague. 1886 moved to Paris where he entered the Cormon studios. Through his brother Theo he became familiar with the paintings of the Impressionists and Neo-Impressionists. February 1888 until May 1889 in Arles, during which period, the happiest of his life, he painted over 200 works. At van Gogh's request Gauguin also came to Arles but left a few months later after van Gogh had tried to attack him with a knife. Entered a lunatic asylum at St. Rémy. 1890 moved to Auvers-sur-Oise where he was treated with great understanding by Dr. Gachet. Another great creative period followed. On 27 July 1890 tried to commit suicide with a revolver, and died of his injuries two days later.

*Literature:* J. Meier-Graefe, Vincent Van Gogh, 2 Bde., München 1921. — L. Piérard, Vincent Van Gogh, Paris 1936. I. Stone, Van Gogh, New York 1936. — G. Schmidt, Van Gogh, Bern 1947. — W. Weisbach, Vincent Van Gogh, Kunst und Schicksal, 2 Bde., Basel 1949—1952. — Ch. Estienne, Van Gogh, Genève 1953. — Vincent Van Gogh, Gesammelte Briefe, 4 Bde., Amsterdam 1953—1954. — Meyer-Schapiro, Vincent Van Gogh, Stuttgart und Zürich 1954. — F. Elagr, Van Gogh, Leben und Werk. München 1959.


## VLAMINCK, MAURICE DE

Born in Paris 4 April 1876. Was a racing-cyclist before he turned to painting in which he received no instruction. Decided to paint after he had seen the 1901 van Gogh exhibition at the Bernheim Gallery. Worked, with Derain, in Chatou, where he met Matisse and subsequently joined the Fauve group. 1905 exhibitions at Berthe Weill and at the Salon d'Automne. Became acquainted with Apollinaire and Picasso. 1908 ceased to paint in the style of the Fauves and until 1914 painted under the influence of Cézanne. 1911 in London; 1913 in Marseilles. 1914—1918 military service. After the war changed to Expressionist compositions. His landscapes, still life and flowerpieces are characterized by heavy brush-strokes. Since 1925 lived in Reuil-la-Gadelière. Also graphic artist and writer. Died in Reuil 11 October 1958.

*Literature:* D. H. Kahnweiler, Maurice de Vlaminck, Leipzig 1920. — F. Fels, Vlaminck, Paris 1928. — W. Grohmann, Vlaminck, Leipzig 1940. — R. Queneau, Maurice de Vlaminck, Genève 1949. — M. Genevoix, Vlaminck, Paris 1954. — M. Sauvage, Vlaminck, sa vie et son message, Genève 1956.


## VUILLARD, EDOUARD

Born in Cuiseaux (Saône-et-Loire) 11 November 1868. 1877 went to Paris where in 1886 he began to study painting under Maillard. 1888 At Julian's where he studied under Bouguereau. 1889 Sérusier, Bonnard, Denis, Vuillard, Roussel, Valloton, Maillol and others founded the "Nabis" group. 1891 first exhibition of his work in the offices of the "Revue Blanche". Shared a studio with Bonnard and Denis, and was influenced by Gauguin and Japanese wood engravings. 1893 decorations for the newly completed Théâtre de l'Oeuvre. Further decorations in the following year for A. Natanson and Dr. Vaquez. 1908 taught at the Académie Ranson. 1913 visited England and Holland with Bonnard. Decorations for Théâtre des Champs Elysées. 1930 visited Spain with Prince Bibesco. 1937—1939 decoration for the Palais de Chaillot in Paris and the League of Nations Building in Geneva. Died in La Baume 21 June 1940. Also graphic artist and lithographer.

*Literature:* C. Roger-Marx, Vuillard et son temps, Paris 1945. — A. Chastel, Vuillard, Paris 1946. — C. Roger-Marx, L'Oeuvre gravé de Vuillard, Monte Carlo 1948. — A. C. Ritchied, Edouard Vuillard, New York 1954. — K. Schweicher, Vuillard, Bern 1955.

# GENERAL LITERATURE

D'Ancona, P., I Classici della pittura italiana del '900, Milano 1953.

Apollinaire, G., Les Peintres cubistes, Paris 1913 (Nouv. éd. Genève 1950).

Apollonio, U., Pittura italiana moderna, Venezia 1950.

Apollonio, U., Pittura metafisica, Venezia 1950.

Bahr, H., Expressionismus, München 1920.

Ball, H., Die Flucht aus der Zeit, 2. Aufl. Luzern 1946.

Ballo, G., Pittori italiani dal futurismo a oggi, Roma 1957.

Barr, A. H. and Hugnet, G., Fantastic Art, Dada, Surrealism, 3rd ed. New York 1947.

Basler, A. et Kunstler, Ch., La peinture indépendante en France, 2 vol. Paris 1929.

Benedetta, Le Futurisme, Paris 1950.

Bo, C., Bilancio del Surrealismo, Padova 1944.

Boccioni, U., Pittura, Scultura futuriste, Dinamismo plastico, Milano 1914.

Breton, A., Le Surréalisme et la peinture, Paris 1928 (Nouv. éd. New York 1945).

Buchheim, L.-G., Die Künstlergemeinschaft Brücke, Feldafing 1956.

Carrà, C., Pittura metafisica, Firenze 1919.

Carrà, C., La mia vita, 2a ed. Milano 1943.

Chassé, Ch., Le Mouvement symboliste dans l'Art du 19e siècle, Paris 1947.

Cheney, S., The Story of Modern Art, New York 1945.

Clark, K., Landscape into Art, London 1949.

Clough, R. T., Looking Back at Futurism, New York 1942.

Coquiot, G., Cubistes, futuristes, passéistes, Paris 1914.

Coquiot, G., Les Indépendants, 1884—1920, 3e éd. Paris 1921.

Costantini, V., Pittura italiana contemporanea, Milano 1934.

Courthion, P., Panorama de la peinture française contemporaine, Paris 1927.

Davidson, M., An Approach to Modern Painting, New York 1948.

Denis, M., Théories, Paris 1913.

Denis, M., Nouvelles Théories, Paris 1921.

Deri, M., Die neue Malerei, Leipzig 1921.

Dorival, B., Les étapes de la peinture française contemporaine, 3 vol., 18e éd. Paris 1948.

Dorival, B., Les peintres du XXe siècle, Paris 1957.

Duplessis, Y., Le surréalisme, Paris 1950.

Duthuit, G., Les Fauves, Genève 1949.

Earp, T. W., The Modern Movement in Painting, London 1935.

Eddy, A. J., Cubists and Post-Impressionism, Chicago 1914.

Einstein, C., Die Kunst des 20. Jahrhunderts (Propyläen-Kunstgeschichte XVI), 3. Aufl. Berlin 1931.

Escholier, R., La peinture française, XXe siècle, Paris 1937.

Faure, E., Histoire de l'art, tome IV, L'art moderne, Paris 1921.

Fechter, P., Der Expressionismus, 3. Aufl. München 1919.

Flora, F., Dal Romanticismo al Futurismo, Milano 1925.

Focillon, H., La peinture aux XIXe et XXe siècles, Paris 1928.

Fontainas, A., Histoire de la peinture française au XIXe siècle, Paris 1906 (Nouv. éd. 1922).

Gleizes, A., Du cubisme et des moyens de la comprendre, Paris 1920.

Habasque, G., Kubismus, Genève 1959.

Haftmann, W., Malerei im 20. Jahrhundert, 2 Bde., München 1954 f.

Hildebrandt, H., Die Kunst des 19. und 20. Jahrhunderts (Handbuch der Kunstwissenschaft), Potsdam 1924.

Huyghe, R., La peinture française, Les contemporains, Notices biographiques par G. Bazin, Paris 1939.

Ironside, R., Painting, an essay in "The New Outline of Modern Knowledge", London 1956.

Janneau, G., L'art cubiste, Paris 1929.

Justi, L., Von Corinth bis Klee, Berlin 1931.

Kahnweiler, D. H., The Rise of Cubism, New York 1949.

Kandinsky, W. und Marc, F., Der Blaue Reiter, München 1912.

Kandinsky, W., Über das Geistige in der Kunst, München 1912.

Kandinsky, W., Punkt und Linie zu Fläche, München 1926.

Klee, P., Pädagogisches Skizzenbuch, München 1925.

Küppers, P. E., Der Kubismus, Leipzig 1920.

Leymarie, J., Fauvismus, Genève 1959.

Marinetti, F. T., Le futurisme, Paris 1911.

Marinetti, F. T., Manifesti del futurismo, Milano 1920—1925.

Meier-Graefe, J., Entwicklungsgeschichte der modernen Kunst, 3 Bde., 4. Aufl. München 1927.

Mondrian, P., Neue Gestaltung, Neoplastizismus, München 1925.

Myers, B. S., Expressionism, London and New York 1957.

Nadeau, M., Histoire du Surréalisme. 2 vol., Paris 1945 ss.

Ozenfant, Foundations of Modern Art, London 1931.

Raynal, M., Histoire de la peinture moderne, tome III, De Picasso au surréalisme, Genève 1950.

Raynal, M., Peinture Moderne, Genève 1953.

Read, H., Surrealism, London 1937.

Roh, F., Nach-Expressionismus, Magischer Realismus, Probleme der neuesten europäischen Malerei, Leipzig 1925.

Röthel, H. K., Moderne deutsche Malerei, Wiesbaden 1957.

Rothenstein, J., Modern English Painters, 2 vol., London 1952 and 1956.

Rutter, F., Evolution in Modern Art, London 1926.

Scheffler, K., Geschichte der europäischen Malerei vom Impressionismus bis zur Gegenwart, Berlin 1927.

Scheiwiller, G., Art italien moderne, Du Futurisme au Novecento, Paris 1930.

Sedlmayr, H., Verlust der Mitte, Salzburg 1948.

Seuphor, M., L'Art abstrait, ses origines, ses premiers maîtres, Paris 1949.

Soby, J. Th. and Barr, A. H., Twentieth-Century Italian Art, New York 1949.

Soffici, A., Cubismo e futurismo, Firenze 1914.

Von Sydow, E., Die deutsche expressionistische Kultur und Malerei, Berlin 1920.

Terrasse, Ch., La peinture française au XXe siècle, Paris 1939.

Thiemen-Becker, Allgemeines Lexikon der bildenden Künstler, Leipzig 1907 ff.

Thoene, P., Modern German Art, London 1938.

Venturi, L., Pittura contemporanea, Milano 1948.

Vollmer, H., Künstlerlexikon des 20. Jahrhunderts, Leipzig 1953 ff.

Walden, H., Einblick in die Kunst; Expressionismus, Futurismus, Kubismus, Berlin 1917.

Walden, H., Expressionismus, Die Kunstwende, Berlin 1918.

Wild, D., Moderne Malerei, Zürich 1950.

Wilenski, R. H., Modern French Painters, London 1945.

Wyss, D., Der Surrealismus. Eine Einführung und Deutung surrealistischer Literatur und Malerei, Heidelberg 1950.

# PLATES

| | | | | | | |
|---|---|---|---|---|---|---|
| 1 | Cézanne | Man with Pipe | about 1892 | Oil | 28³/₄ x 23⁵/₈ in. | Courtauld Institute, London |
| 2 | Cézanne | Still Life with Onions | 1895—1900 | Oil | 26 x 31⁷/₈ in. | Musée du Louvre, Paris |
| 3 | Van Gogh | Portrait of Dr. Gachet | 1890 | Oil | 26³/₄ x 22⁷/₁₆ in. | Musée de l'Impressionnisme, Paris |
| 4 | Cézanne | Le Cabanon de Jourdan | 1906 | Oil | 25³/₄ x 32 in. | Private Collection, Deposit Kunstmuseum Basel |
| 5 | Van Gogh | Peach-trees in Blossom near Arles | 1889 | Oil | 25³/₄ x 32 in. | Courtauld Institute, London |
| 6 | Gauguin | Nafea Faa ipoipo | 1892 | Oil | 40 x 30¹/₂ in. | Collection R. Staechelin, Deposit Kunstmuseum Basel |
| 7 | Bonnard | Nude in false Light | about 1908 | Oil | 49¹/₄ x 43 in. | Musées Royaux des B.-A., Bruxelles |
| 8 | Bonnard | Signac and his Friends, Sailing | 1926/28 | Oil | 49 x 54³/₄ in. | Kunsthaus, Zürich |
| 9 | Vuillard | Draughts | 1906 | Oil | 29⁷/₈ x 43 in. | Coll. Prof. Dr. H. R. Hahnloser, Bern |
| 10 | Vuillard | Interior | 1896 | Oil | 83⁷/₈ x 60⁵/₈ in. | Petit Palais, Paris |
| 11 | Denis | The Muses | 1893 | Oil | 66³/₁₆ x 53³/₁₆ in. | Musée National d'Art moderne, Paris |
| 12 | Toulouse-Lautrec | Woman making her toilet | 1896 | Oil | 25¹/₂ x 20⁷/₈ in. | Musée du Louvre, Paris |
| 13 | Ensor | Objects in a Studio | 1889 | Oil | 33¹/₂ x 45⁵/₁₆ in. | Coll. Roland Leten, Gand |
| 14 | Munch | Music in the Street | 1889 | Oil | 40³/₁₆ x 55³/₄ in. | Kunsthaus, Zürich |
| 15 | Hodler | Self-Portrait | 1891 | Oil | 11³/₁₆ x 9¹/₁₆ in. | Gottfried-Keller-Stiftung Deposit Musée d'Art et d'Histoire, Genève |
| 16 | Munch | Girls on the Bridge | 1899 | Oil | 54 x 49⁵/₈ in. | Nationalgalerie, Oslo |
| 17 | Hodler | Landscape "Jungfrau" | 1914 | Oil | 24⁵/₈ x 32⁵/₈ in. | Musée d'Art et d'Histoire, Genève |
| 18 | Matisse | Portrait of Margaret | 1906 | Oil | 25³/₁₆ x 35⁷/₁₆ in. | Musée des Beaux-Arts, Grenoble |
| 19 | Matisse | Still Life with Magnolia | 1941 | Oil | 28³/₄ x 39³/₈ in. | Musée National d'Art moderne, Paris |
| 20 | Matisse | Interior with Violin | 1917—18 | Oil | 45³/₄ x 35 in. | Statens Museum for Kunst, Collection J. Rump, Copenhagen |
| 21 | Matisse | Decorative Figure on Ornamental Back- [ground | 1927 | Oil | 51¹/₄ x 38⁵/₈ in. | Musée National d'Art moderne, Paris |
| 22 | Vlaminck | The Red Trees | 1906 | Oil | 25¹/₂ x 31⁷/₈ in. | Musée National d'Art moderne, Paris |
| 23 | Dufy | Port of Le Havre | 1906 | Oil | 23⁵/₈ x 28³/₄ in. | Musée des Beaux-Arts, Nantes |
| 24 | Dufy | Nice, La Baie des Anges | 1927 | Oil | 31⁷/₈ x 39³/₈ in. | Coll. Ph. Dotremont, Bruxelles |
| 25 | Marquet | The Horse, Marseille | 1916 | Oil | 25¹/₂ x 31⁷/₈ in. | Coll. Marcelle Marquet, Paris |
| 26 | Derain | The Road to Beauvais | 1911 | Oil | 19⁷/₈ x 24 in. | Coll. Hermann und Margrit Rupf, Bern |
| 27 | Rouault | The Holy Face | 1933 | Oil | 35⁷/₈ x 25¹/₂ in. | Musée National d'Art moderne, Paris |
| 28 | Derain | Blackfriars | 1907 | Oil | 32 x 39 in. | Art Gallery, Glasgow |
| 29 | Rouault | Biblical Landscape | 1933/36 | Oil | 27¹/₈ x 21¹/₄ in. | Petit Palais, Coll. Girardin, Paris |
| 30 | Utrillo | The Gate St. Martin | 1909/10 | Oil | 29⁷/₈ x 36 in. | Tate Gallery, London |
| 31 | Chagall | The Jew | 1914 | Oil | 39³/₈ x 31¹/₂ in. | Coll. Charles Im Obersteg, Genève |
| 32 | Chagall | I and the Village | 1911 | Oil | 75⁵/₈ x 59⁵/₈ in. | Museum of Modern Art, New York Mrs. Simon Guggenheim Fund |
| 33 | Utrillo | La Fère en Tardenois | 1912 | Oil | 31⁷/₈ x 23⁵/₈ in. | Petit Palais, Coll. Girardin, Paris |
| 34 | Modigliani | Sitting Nude "La Romana" | 1917 | Oil | 39³/₈ x 25¹/₂ in. | Coll. Georges Renand, Paris |
| 35 | Modersohn | Sitting Child with Flowers | 1907 | Oil | 35⁷/₈ x 43³/₈ in. | Städtisches Museum, Wuppertal |
| 36 | Modersohn | Still Life with Melon | 1905 | Oil | 27¹/₈ x 35⁷/₁₆ in. | Wallraf-Richartz Museum, Köln |
| 37 | Soutine | English Woman | about 1922 | Oil | 20⁷/₈ x 13 in. | Coll. Charles Im Obersteg, Genève |
| 38 | Kirchner | Variety | 1907 | Oil | 59¹/₂ x 47¹/₄ in. | Private Collection, Germany |
| 39 | Pechstein | The Green House | 1909 | Oil | 29¹/₂ x 29¹/₂ in. | Wallraf-Richartz Museum, Köln |
| 40 | Heckel | Port in Göteborg | 1928 | Oil | 37³/₄ x 47¹/₂ in. | Wallraf-Richartz Museum, Köln |
| 41 | Schmidt-Rottluff | Summer | 1913 | Oil | 34⁵/₈ x 41 in. | Landesgalerie, Hannover |
| 42 | Beckmann | Robbery of Europe | 1933 | Water-colour | 20¹/₁₆ x 27¹/₂ in. | Coll. Lilly v. Schnitzler, Frankfurt a. M. |
| 43 | Nolde | Christ and the Sinner | 1926 | Oil | 33⁷/₈ x 42¹/₈ in. | Coll. Prof. Dr. H. Fehr, Muri bei Bern |
| 44 | Kokoschka | Leuk, View of the Rhone Valley | 1947 | Oil | 29¹/₂ x 39³/₈ in. | Coll. Adolf Ratjen, Vaduz |
| 45 | Beckmann | Reclining Woman with Mandolin | 1950 | Oil | 36 x 55 in. | Galerie Otto Stangl, München |
| 46 | Picasso | Child with Pigeon | 1901 | Oil | 28³/₄ x 21¹/₄ in. | Coll. Lady Aberconway, London |
| 47 | Picasso | The Guitar | 1920 | Oil | 25³/₄ x 36³/₈ in. | Öffentliche Kunstsammlung, Basel, Emanuel-Hoffmann-Stiftung |
| 48 | Picasso | Still Life with Cooking Pot | 1945 | Oil | 32¹/₄ x 41³/₄ in. | Musée National d'Art moderne, Paris |
| 49 | Picasso | Harlequin | 1923 | Oil | 49⁵/₈ x 37³/₄ in. | Coll. Charles Im Obersteg, Genève |
| 50 | Braque | Landscape | 1908 | Oil | 37⁷/₈ x 25⁵/₈ in. | Öffentliche Kunstsammlung, Basel |

| 51 | Gris | Ravignan Square | 1915 | Oil | $45^3/4$ x 35 | in. | Philadelphia Museum of Art, W. and L. Arensberg Coll., Philadelphia USA |
|----|------|-----------------|------|-----|----|----|----|
| 52 | Braque | Still Life | 1926 | Oil | 19 x 23 | in. | Art Gallery, Glasgow |
| 53 | Gris | Le Canigou | 1921 | Oil | $25^5/8$ x $39^3/8$ | in. | Albright Art Gallery, Buffalo USA |
| 54 | Léger | Staircase | 1913 | Oil | $56^3/4$ x $46^1/2$ | in. | Kunsthaus, Zürich |
| 55 | Delaunay | Eiffel Tower | 1910 | Oil | 77 x $50^3/4$ | in. | Öffentliche Kunstsammlung, Basel, Emanuel-Hoffmann-Stiftung |
| 56 | Delaunay | Still Life Portuguese | 1917 | Oil | $68^7/8$ x $84^1/4$ | in. | Coll. Dr. Franz Meyer, Zürich |
| 57 | Léger | Three Women | 1921 | Oil | $72^1/4$ x 99 | in. | Museum of Modern Art, New York Mrs. Simon Guggenheim Fund |
| 58 | Severini | The Boulevard | 1910 | Oil | $25^3/4$ x $36^1/4$ | in. | Coll. E. Estorick, London |
| 59 | De Chirico | Hector and Andromache | 1917 | Oil | $35^7/16$ x $23^5/8$ | in. | Coll. Gianni Mattioli, Milano |
| 60 | Boccioni | States of Mind I., "The Farewells" | 1911 | Oil | $26^3/4$ x $37^3/8$ | in. | Private Collection, USA |
| 61 | Carrà | Solitude | 1917 | Oil | $35^7/16$ x $23^5/8$ | in. | Coll. Dr. Giedion-Welcker, Zürich |
| 62 | Carrà | The Canal | 1926 | Oil | $16^3/4$ x $20^1/4$ | in. | Kunsthaus, Zürich |
| 63 | Klee | Twittering Machine | 1922 | Water-colour, oil and pen | $16^1/4$ x 12 | in. | Museum of Modern Art, New York |
| 64 | Klee | Fish Magic | 1925 | Oil and water-colour | $30^5/16$ x $38^5/8$ | in. | Philadelphia Museum of Art, Arensberg Collection |
| 65 | Klee | Visionary Birdman | about 1930 | Pastel | $18^1/8$ x $12^3/16$ | in. | Coll. Nika Hulton, London |
| 66 | Klee | Bastard | 1939 | Oil and tempera | $23^5/8$ x $27^1/2$ | in. | Coll. Felix Klee, Bern |
| 67 | Kandinsky | Improvisation 35 | 1914 | Oil | $43^3/8$ x $47^1/4$ | in. | Coll. Hans Arp, Meudon |
| 68 | Kandinsky | Improvisation 9 | 1910 | Oil | $43^3/8$ x $43^3/8$ | in. | Private Collection, Zürich |
| 69 | Kandinsky | Triangles in a Curve | 1927 | Oil | 26 x $19^1/4$ | in. | Private Collection, München |
| 70 | Kandinsky | Elan brun | 1943 | Oil | $16^1/2$ x $22^7/8$ | in. | Coll. Mme. Nina Kandinsky, Paris |
| 71 | Marc | The Gazelle | 1912 | Water-colour | 14 x $17^1/4$ | in. | Museum of Art, Rhode Island School of Design, Providence 3, Rhode Island USA |
| 72 | Campigli | The Brides of the Sailors | 1934 | Oil | $28^3/4$ x $34^5/8$ | in. | Galleria d'Arte Moderna, Roma |
| 73 | Marc | Three Horses | 1912 | Oil | $29^7/8$ x $35^3/8$ | in. | Coll. Emil Bührle, Zürich |
| 74 | Schlemmer | Bauhaus-Staircase | about 1929 | Oil | $63^3/4$ x $44^3/4$ | in. | Museum of Modern Art, New York |
| 75 | Feininger | The Cyclists | 1912 | Oil | $31^3/4$ x $39^3/8$ | in. | Coll. Frau Maria Möller, Köln |
| 76 | Feininger | Church in Halle | 1930 | Oil | $40^1/8$ x $31^3/4$ | in. | Bayerische Staatsgemäldesammlung, München |
| 77 | Macke | Walkers on the Bridge | 1912 | Oil | $33^7/8$ x $39^3/8$ | in. | Hessisches Landesmuseum, Darmstadt |
| 78 | Nicholson | Still Life | 1931—36 | Oil | $26^3/4$ x 30 | in. | British Council, London |
| 79 | Tanguy | The Five Strangers | 1941 | Oil | $39^1/8$ x $31^5/8$ | in. | Wadsworth Atheneum, Hartford USA |
| 80 | Dali | Burning Giraffe | 1935 | Oil | $13^3/4$ x $10^5/8$ | in. | Öffentliche Kunstsammlung, Basel, Emanuel-Hoffmann-Stiftung |
| 81 | Miró | Carnival of the Harlequin | 1924/25 | Oil | 26 x $36^5/8$ | in. | Albright Art Gallery, Buffalo USA |
| 82 | Ernst | Celebes | 1921 | Oil | $51^1/4$ x $34^3/8$ | in. | Coll. Roland Penrose, London |
| 83 | John | Robin | 1909 | Oil | 18 x 14 | in. | Tate Gallery, London |
| 84 | Rivera | The Flower Vendor | 1935 | Oil | 48 x 48 | in. | San Francisco Museum of Art, San Francisco USA |
| 85 | Smith | Peaches | 1940 | Oil | $23^1/2$ x $28^1/2$ | in. | Tate Gallery, London |
| 86 | Spencer | Christ Carrying the Cross | 1920 | Oil | 60 x 56 | in. | Tate Gallery, London |
| 87 | Jones | Illustration to the Arthurian Legend: The Four Queens | 1941 | Pen and water-colour | $24^1/2$ x $19^1/2$ | in. | Tate Gallery, London |
| 88 | Sutherland | Entrance to a Lane | 1939 | Oil | $23^1/2$ x $19^1/2$ | in. | Tate Gallery, London |
| 89 | Gilman | Mrs. Mounter at the Breakfast Table | 1916 | Oil | $23^1/2$ x $15^1/2$ | in. | Tate Gallery, London |
| 90 | Nash | Pillar and Moon | 1932—42 | Oil | 20 x 30 | in. | Tate Gallery, London |
| 91 | Demuth | Aucassin and Nicoletta | 1921 | Oil | $23^5/8$ x $19^1/2$ | in. | Columbus Gallery of Fine Arts, Coll. of Ferdinand Howald, Columbus, Ohio USA |
| 92 | Bacon | Figure in a Landscape | 1946 | Oil | 57 x $50^1/2$ | in. | Tate Gallery, London |
| 93 | Lewis | Edith Sitwell | 1923—35 | Oil | 34 x 44 | in. | Tate Gallery, London |
| 94 | Moore | Two Seated Women | 1940 | Pen, ink and water-colour | $7^1/8$ x $10^5/8$ | in. | Tate Gallery, London |
| 95 | Marin | City Construction | 1932 | Water-colour | 26 x $21^1/4$ | in. | Albright Art Gallery, Buffalo USA |
| 96 | Mondrian | Plate I. | 1921 | Oil | 38 x $23^3/4$ | in. | Coll. Dr. O. Müller-Widmann, Basel |

Photos, negatives and colour separations were supplied by:

Photographisches Atelier Hinz, Basel
Öffentliche Kunstsammlung, Basel
Peter Moeschlin, Basel
Dietrich Widmer, Basel
Kurt Blum, Bern
Martin Hesse, Bern
Albright Art Gallery, Buffalo, USA
The Columbus Gallery of Fine Arts, Columbus, Ohio, USA
Städelsches Kunstinstitut, Frankfurt am Main
Charles Pricam, Genève
Scottish Studios & Engravers Ltd., Glasgow
Studio Piccardy, Grenoble
Landesgalerie, Hannover
Wadsworth Atheneum, Hartford, USA
Lichtbildanstalt Hermann Claasen, Köln
Bildarchiv, Rheinisches Museum, Köln
Dr. Wolfgang Salchow, Köln
Statens Museum for Kunst, Kopenhagen
Courtauld Institute, London
Fine Art Engravers Ltd., London
R. B. Fleming & Co. Ltd., London
Nika Hulton, London
Tate Gallery, London
Gianni Mari, Milano
Musée des Beaux-Arts, Nantes
Museum of Modern Art, New York
Charles Uht, New York
Cliché Mauritz Iversen, Oslo
Archives Photographiques, Paris
Photo Bulloz, Paris
Mario Lazzari, Paris
Philadelphia Museum of Art, Philadelphia
Museum of Art, Rhode Island School of Design, Rhode Island, Providence, USA
De Antonis, Roma
M. Halberstadt, San Francisco
Foto Giacomelli, Venezia
Helmut Vooes, Wuppertal-Elberfeld
Fachschriftenverlag, Zürich
Walter Dräyer, Zürich
Gottfried-Keller-Stiftung, Zürich
Kunsthaus, Zürich
Schwitter AG, Zürich

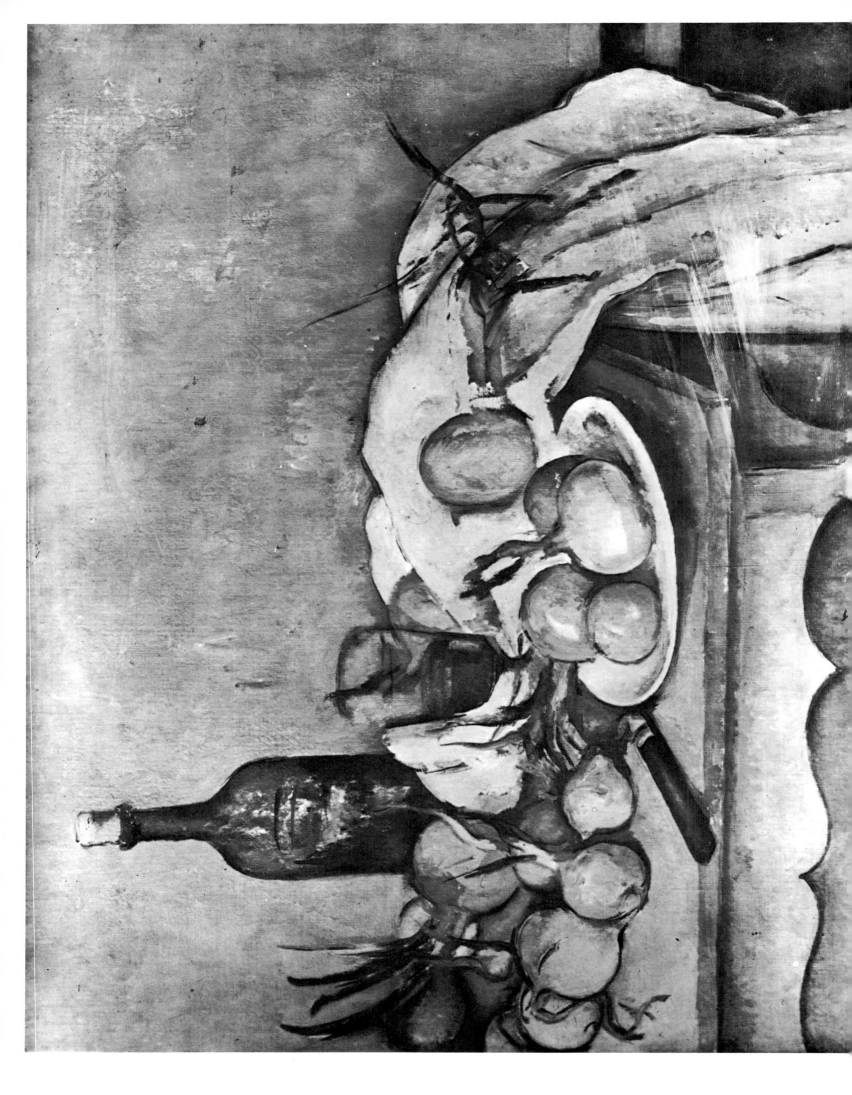

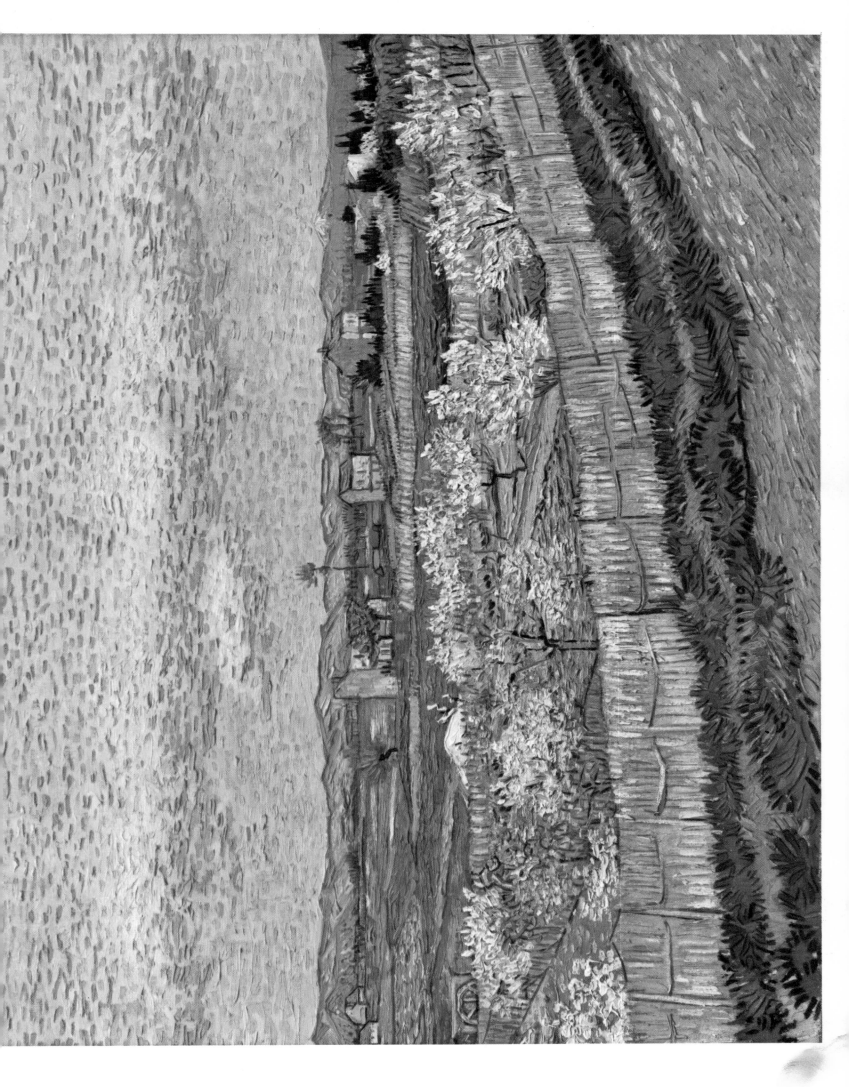

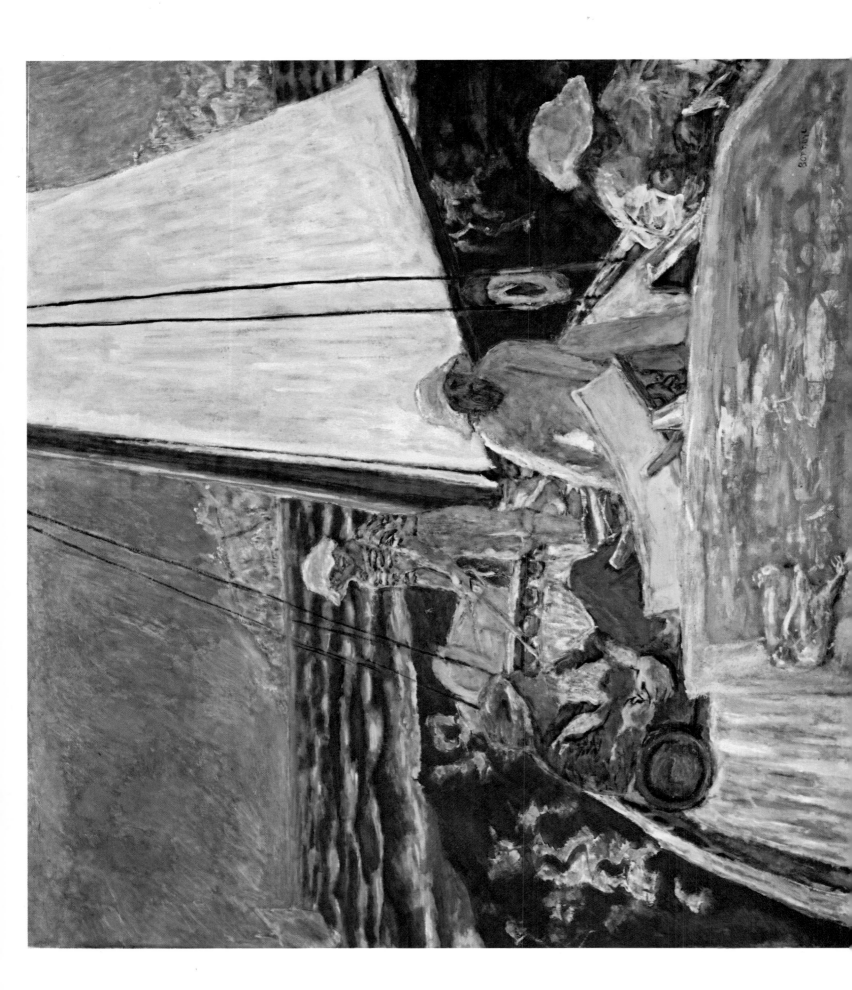

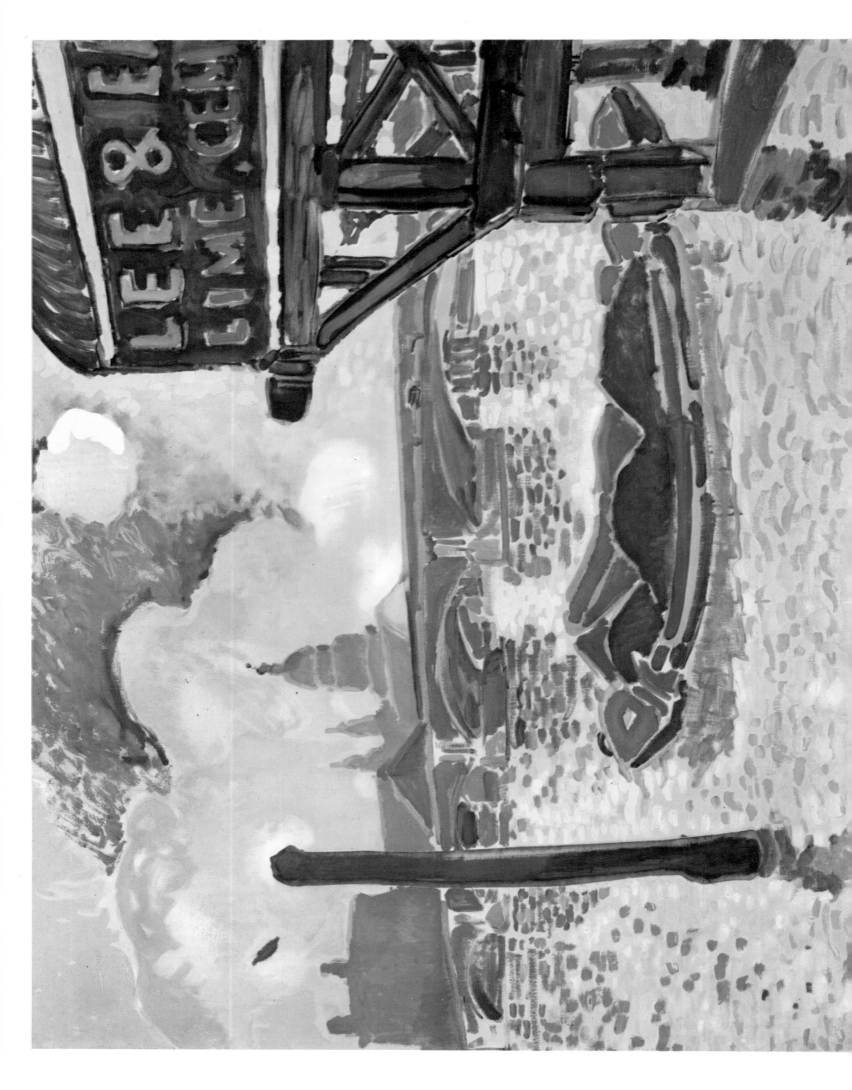

Maurice Utrillo. V.

EMIL NOLDE 43

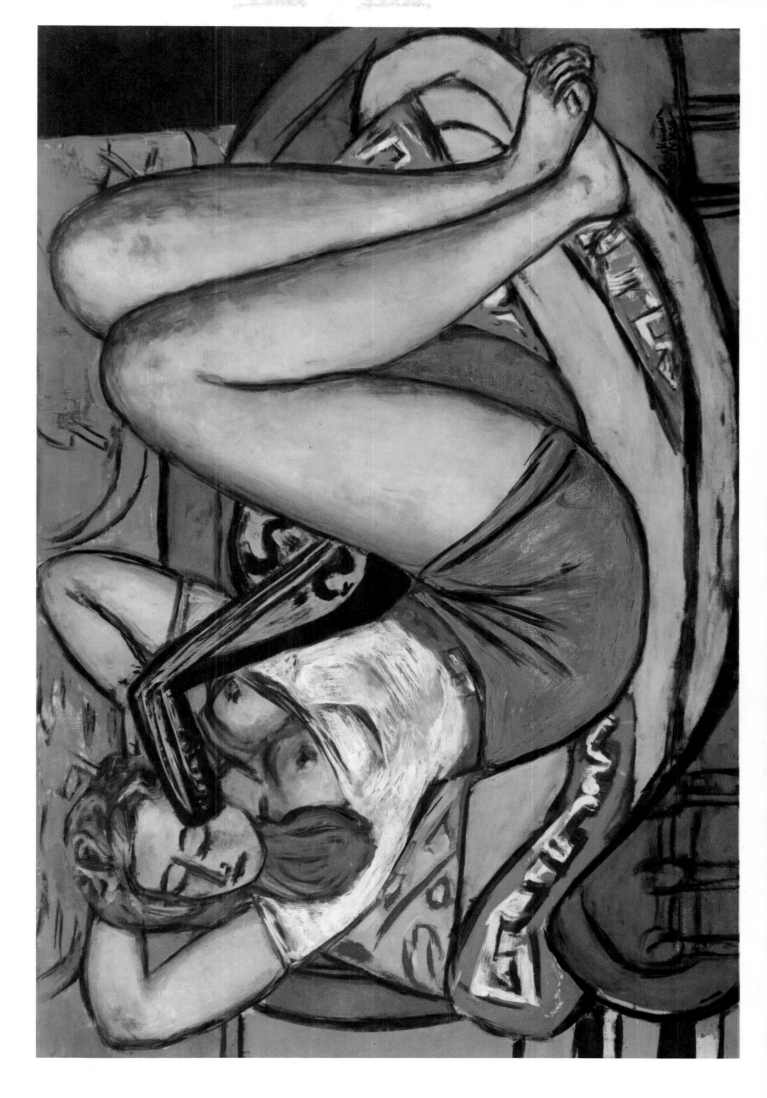

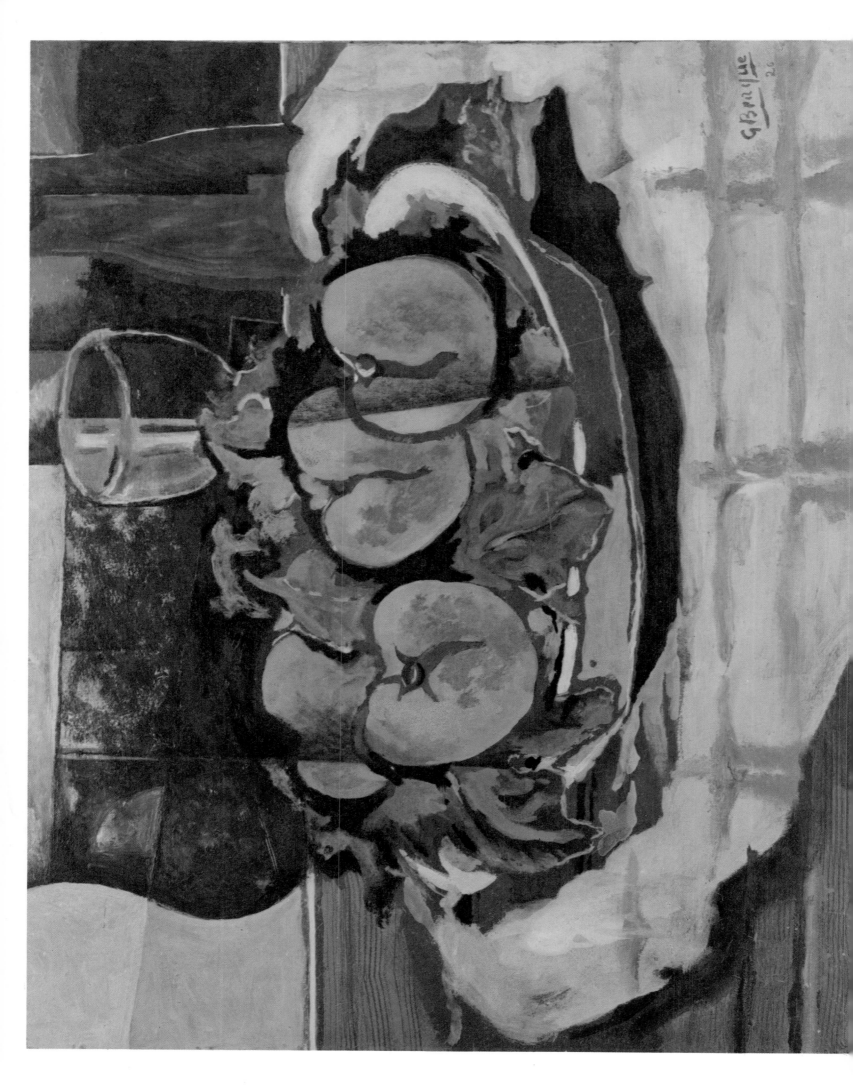

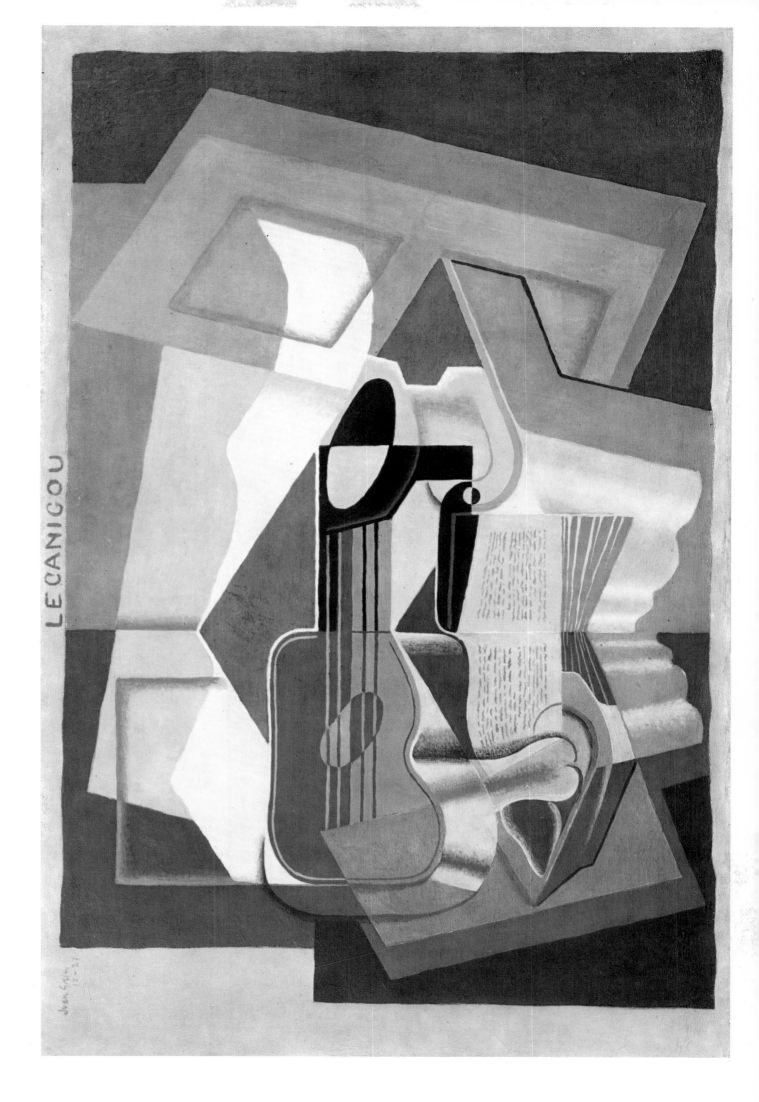

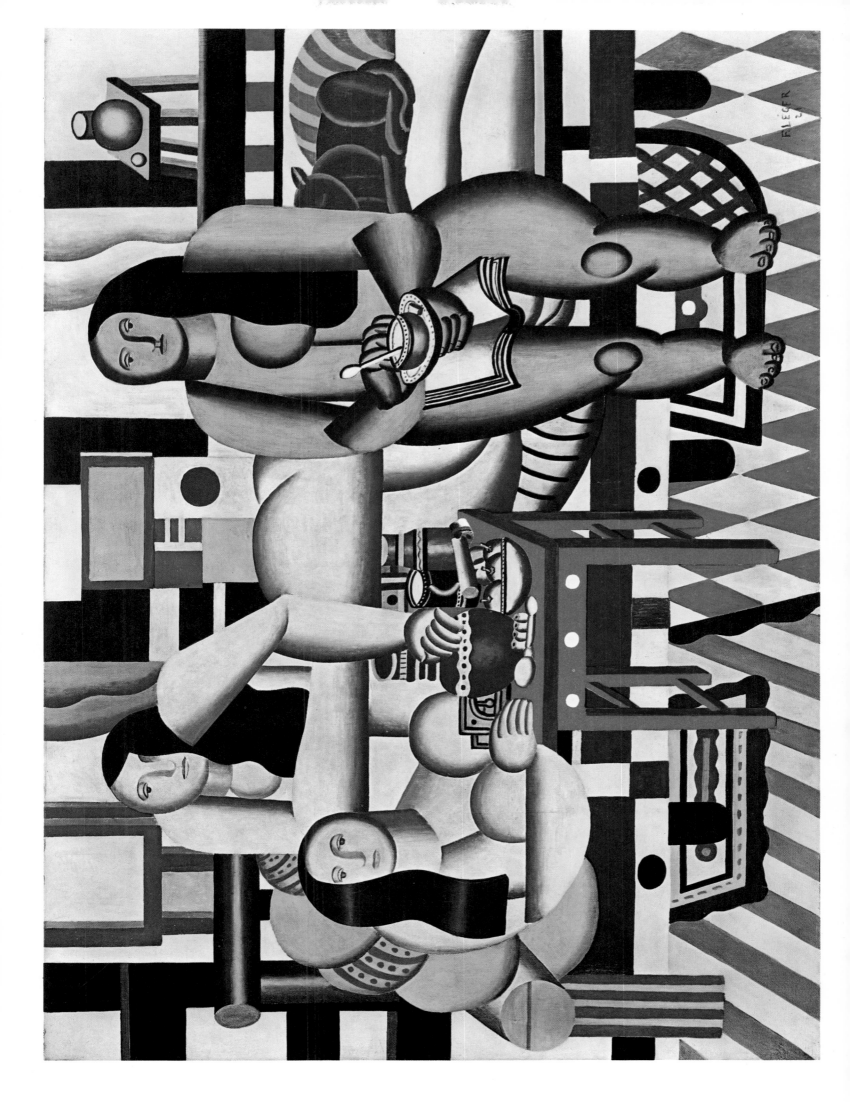

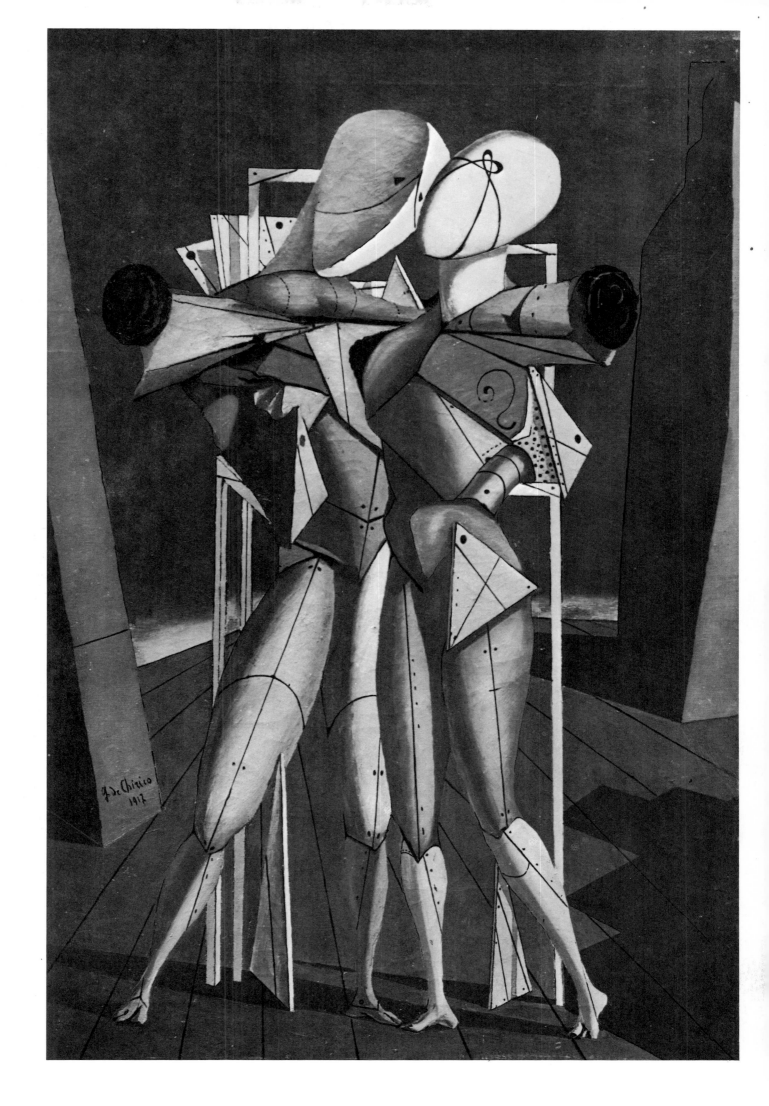

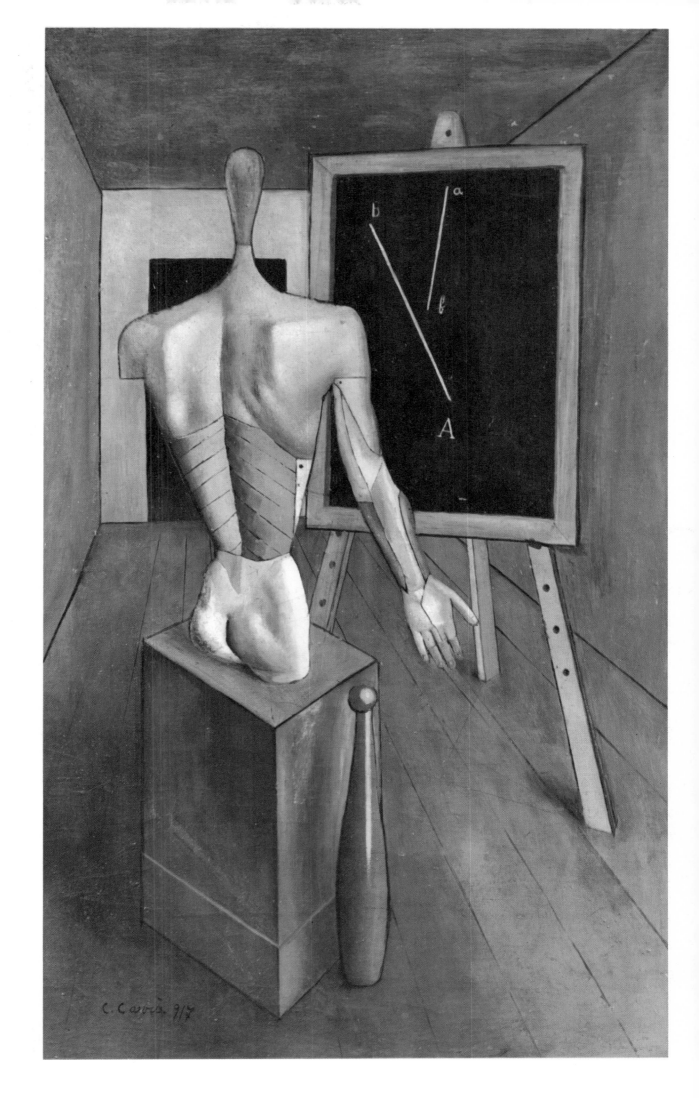

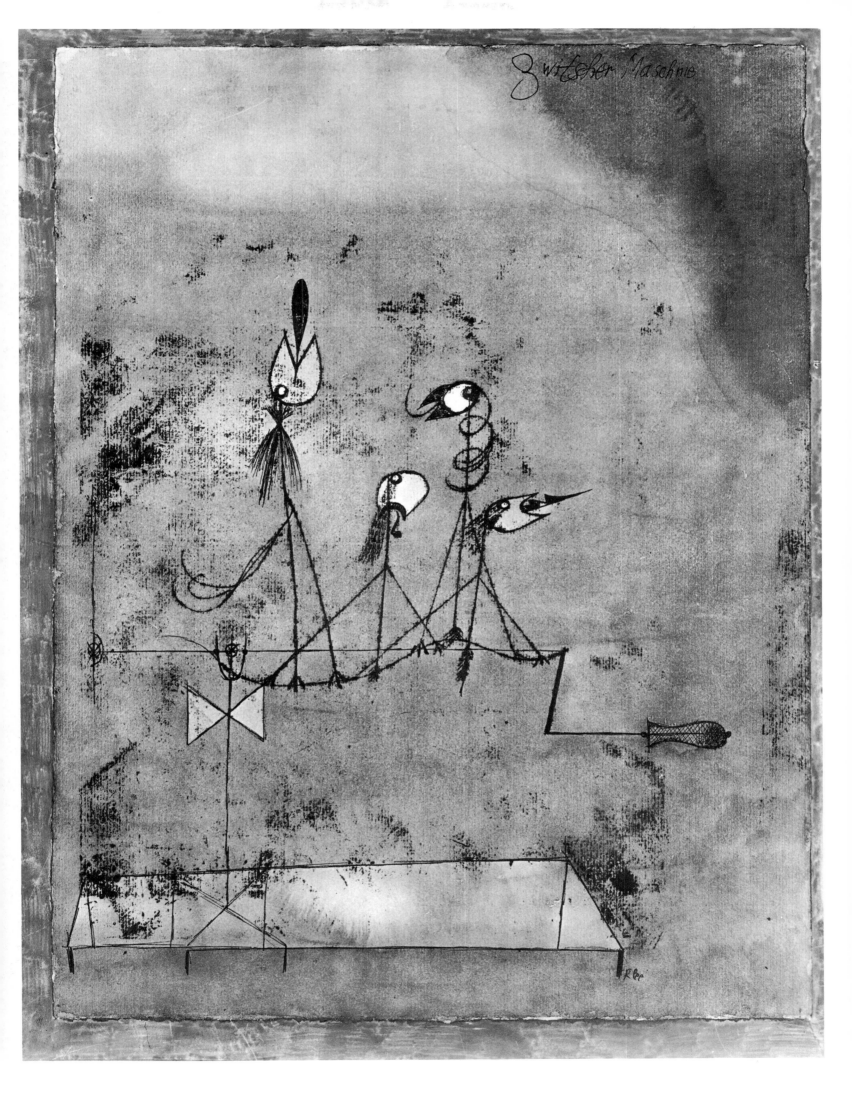

*Zwitscher Maschine*

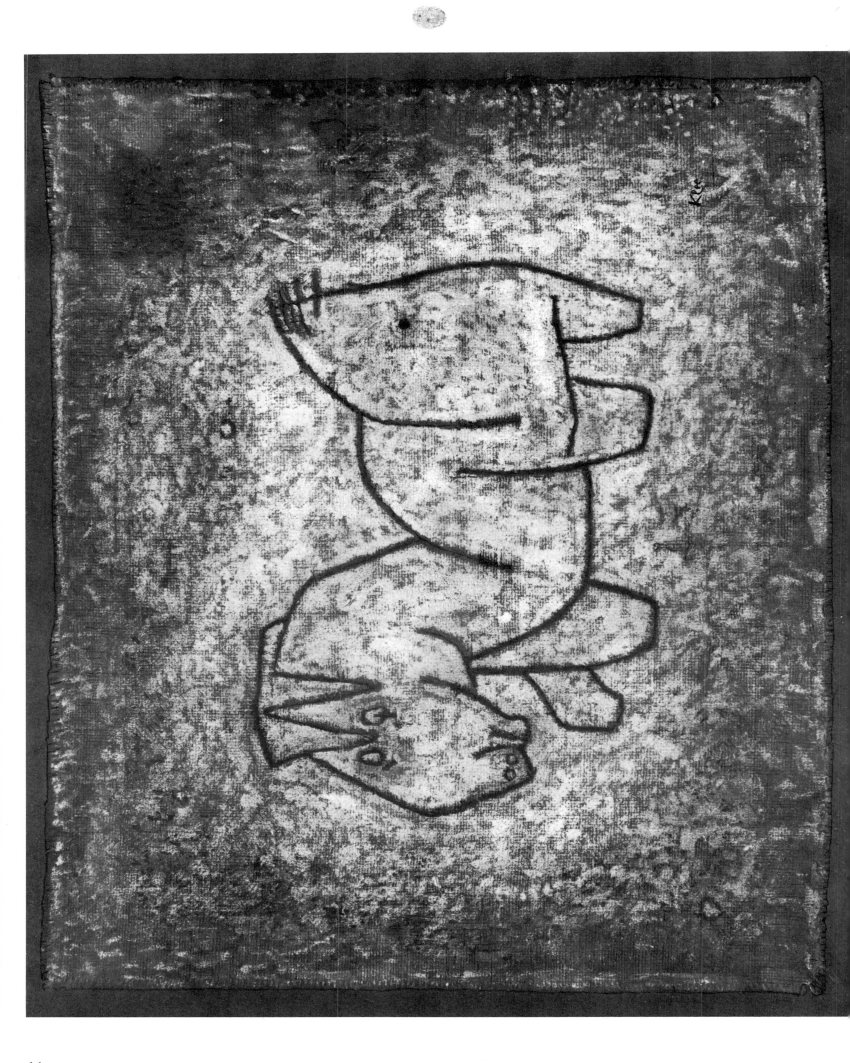

66 PAUL KLEE

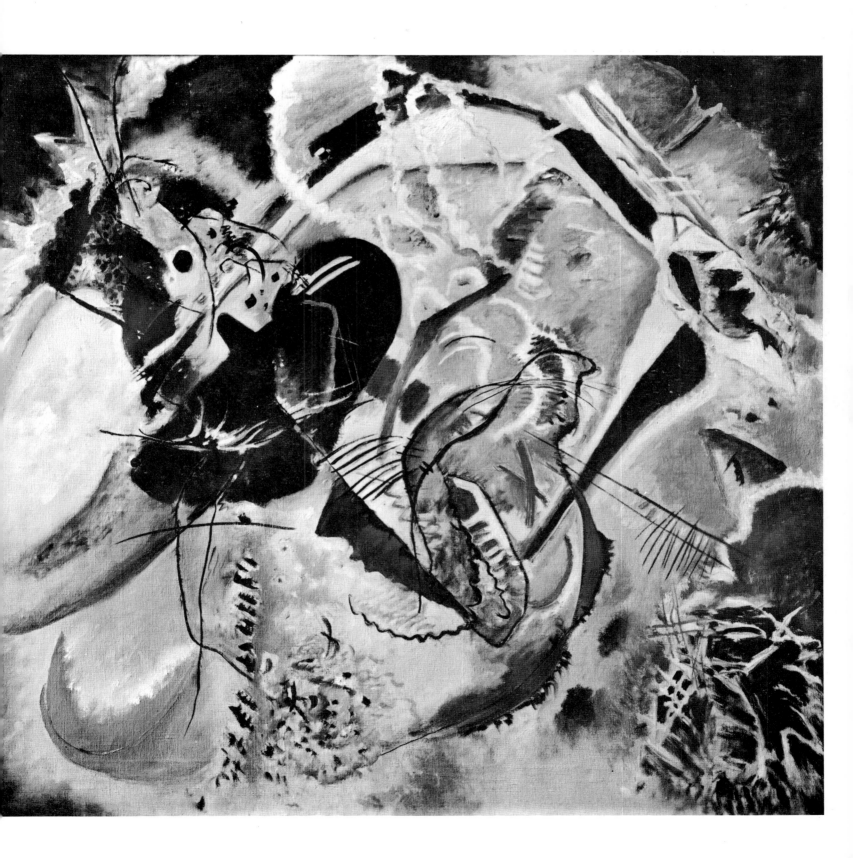

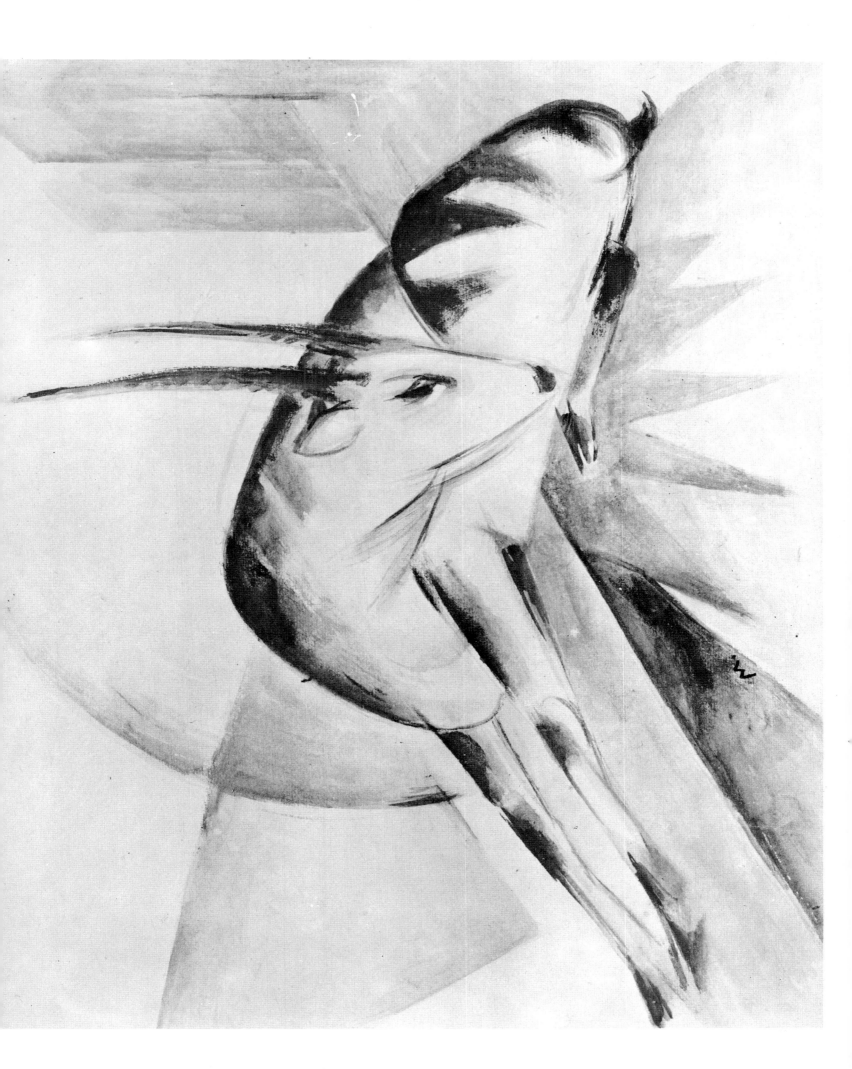

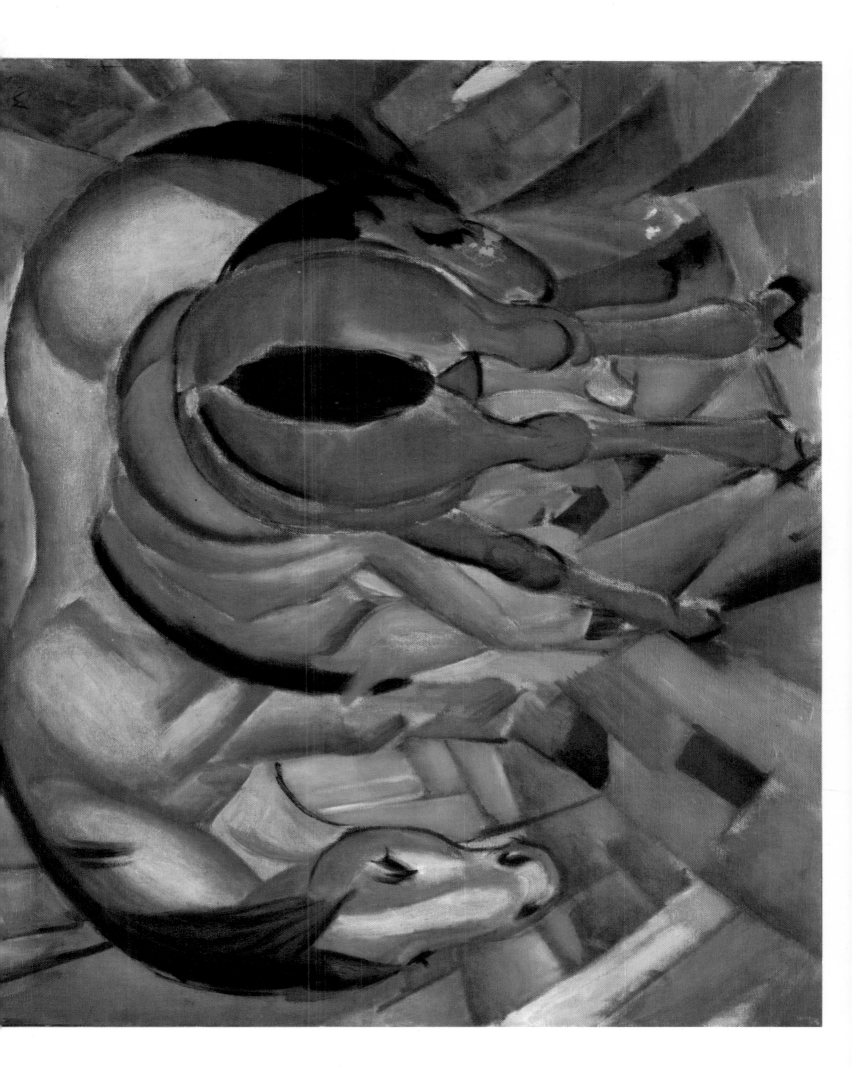

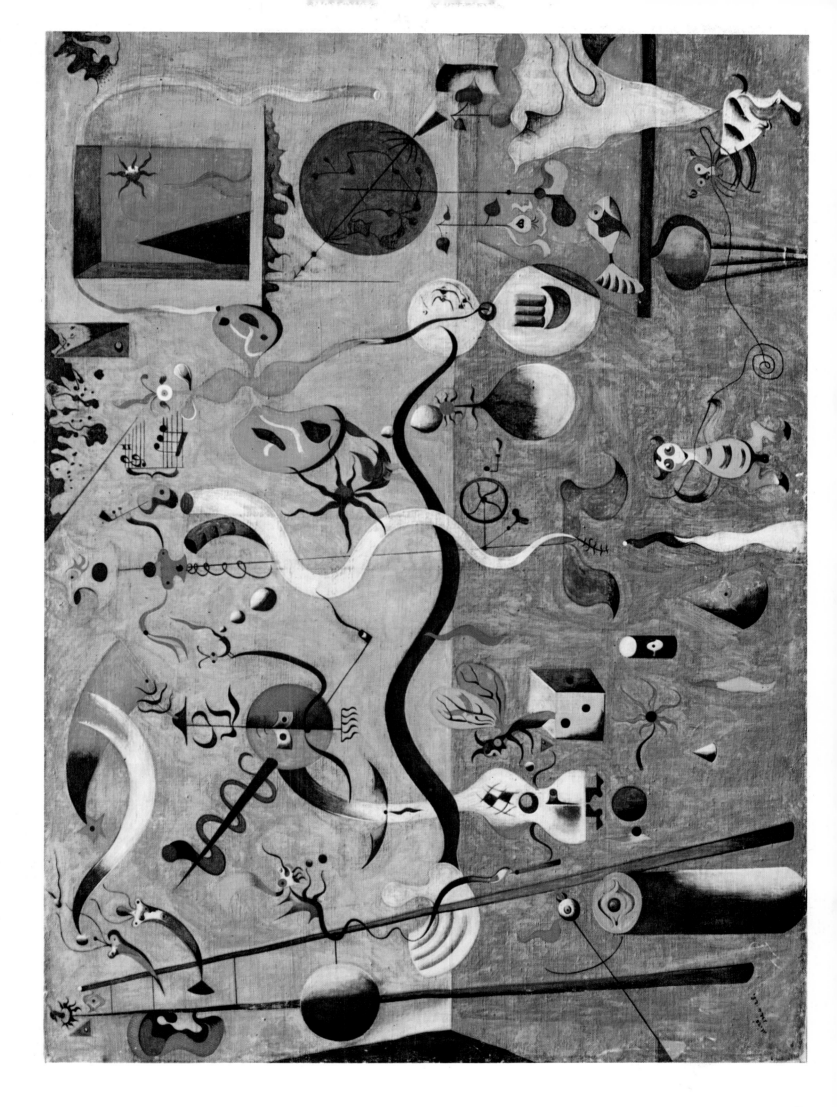

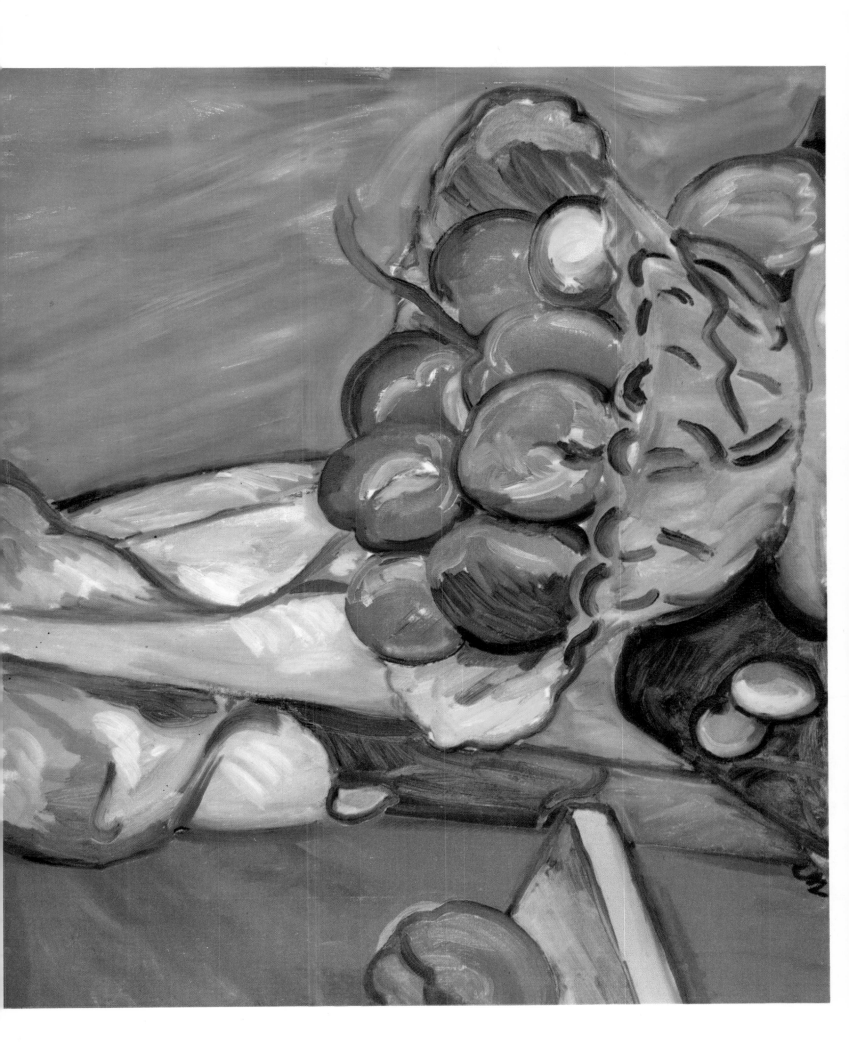

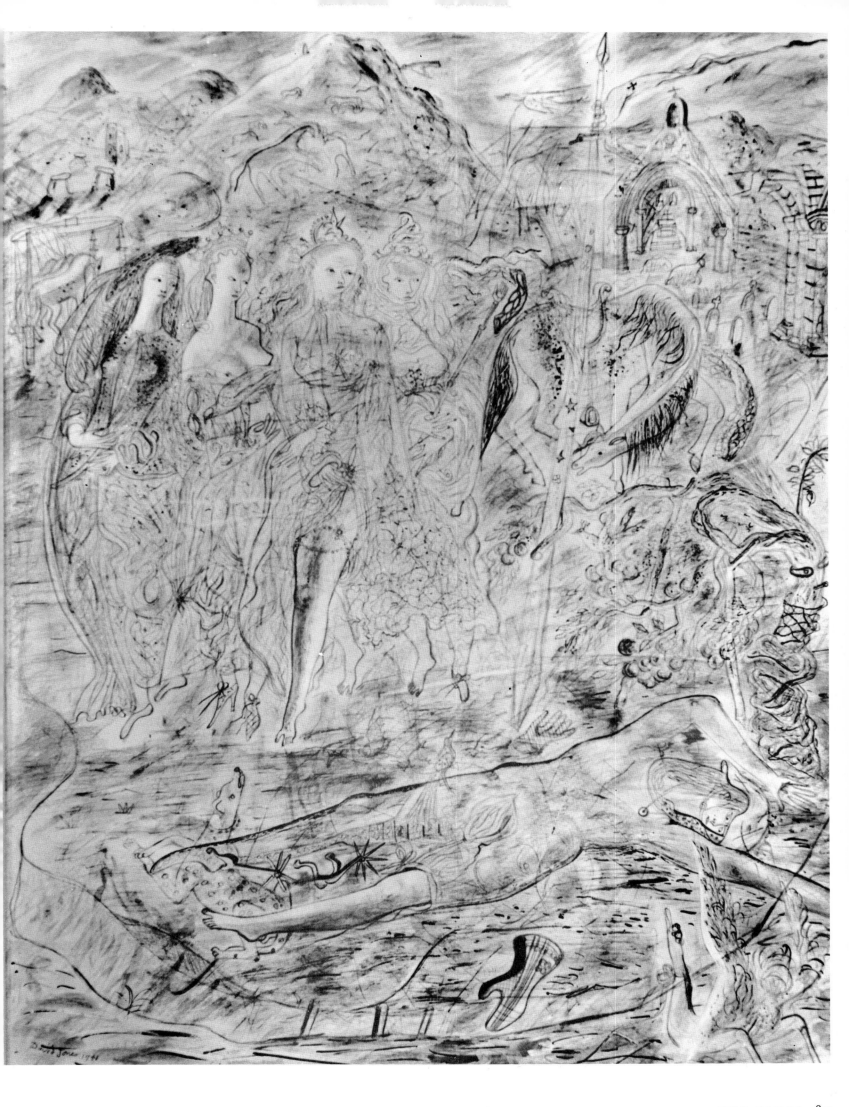